This book is dedicated to my son
ELI-GRAEME

Recipes compiled by:
101 ways to COOK MARRON &
The TRUE MARRON 1.0.1 2002-2023
First Publication 2023
South West Print & Design
Manjimup, Western Australia 6258

All rights reserved. No part of this Publication may be reproduced, stored in a retrieval system, transmitted in any form or by any means, electronic, mechanical, photocopying, recording or otherwise without written permission of the Copyright Owner and Publisher.

**FOR MORE INFORMATION OR TO FIND OUT HOW TO
BE A PART OF FUTURE PUBLICATIONS
GO TO: THETRUEMARRON101.AU**

"WE ACKNOWLEDGE THE TRADITIONAL CUSTODIANS OF THE LAND ON WHICH WE GATHER,
WE RECOGNISE THEIR CONTINUED CONNECTION TO THE LAND AND WATERS OF THIS BEAUTIFUL PLACE AND
ACKNOWLEDGE ANY FIRST NATIONS PEOPLE READING OUR BOOK AND ACKNOWLEDGED IN THESE PAGES.

AN INTRODUCTION TO MARRON 10

Can't just have you diving face first now can we?

WHAT ARE THESE BUG-GERS?	11
YOU CAN'T MAKE THIS STUFF UP!	12
THEIR ROLE IN THE ECOSYSTEM	13
YABBIES SPREAD BY UNDERGROUND CREEKS	14
BORN CRAY-Z AWARD - MICK DE WIT	14
WHAT'S HAPPENED TO OUR LOCAL SPECIES?	16
PARTICIPATION AWARD - MERRELL BURNETT	17
GEOLOGY OF THE SOUTH-WEST REGIONS	18
THE BIGGER, THE OLDER, THE DEEPER?	18
OUT COMPETED BY EARLY BREEDING CYCLES	20
BAR GRAPH OF BREEDING RESULTS	21
WHAT IS UNDER THAT HARD SHELL?	22
WHAT DO I HAVE IN MY NET?	22
WHAT SEX IS MY CRAYFISH?	24
HAIRY MARRON - MOSSYBACK	26
SMOOTH MARRON	27
KOONAC	28
GILGIE	29
DIL / FRESHWATER BURROWING CRAYFISH	30
YABBY	31
'POLYPS' IT'S A GASTROLITH	32
THE TASTIEST LINE UP EVA	34
WOODVALE FISH & LILY FARM - CALINDA ANDERSON	36
THE WOODVALE FISH & LILY FARM TEAM	37
SURRENDER UNWANTED FISH	37
ALGAE, WHAT'S IT ALL ABOUT?	38
WE REWARD YOU FOR GIVING YOUR CRAY THE BEST!	39
HOW MUCH TO FEED YOU ASK?	39

KEEPING CRAYFISH 36

If you are going to get a pet, take the effort to take care of it properly. Also feeding it what it needs. Not Catfood.

WHAT ELSE CAN I FEED MY CRAY?	40
A PART OF THE FAMILY	41
PARTICIPATION AWARD - IAN MITCHELL	42
GET THE RIGHT TANK FOR YOUR CRAYFISH	43
FROM HARDCASE TO ABSOLUTE SOFTY	45
DR. DULANA HERATH & PASES AQUA - WA	46
AN 'INTERACTIVE' PET FOR ALL AGES	47
RULER OF THE TANK	48
A GRAMMATICAL ERROR IN TRANSLATIONS OVER TIME?	48

MEAT THE CONTESTANTS & JUDGES — 50

'MEAT' Hahaha Sorry, easy pun! Meet the CREW behind the book.

MEAT THE CONTESTANTS	6
MEAT MAZZ - OUR HEAD JUDGE	50
MEAT ALUNIO - MAZZ'S 'MUSCLE'	52
MEAT COBBA - NOT A CAT-FISH	54
MEAT TROUDY - OUR LOCAL 'CELERY'ITY JUDGE	94
MEAT CSIRAX - YABBY DABBA DOO'S 'CELERY'ITY JUDGE	175

PREPARING YOUR CRAYFISH — 56

Some quick and simple advice about getting the most flavour from your marron or other crayfish, regardless of size.

HOW DO YOU COOK A CRAYFISH?	56
PARTICIPATION AWARD - MATT SMITH	58
DEFROSTING	58
YOU CAN LEAVE YOUR FLAP ON!	58
GETTING RID OF THE GOOEY BIT	58
THIS TOPIC BRINGS ME TO BOILING POINT!	59
SO, LET'S MAKE IT EASY!	59
EXTRACTING THE FLESH	60
BUTTERFLYING	60
SPLITTING IN HALF (COOKED OR UNCOOKED)	60
SHOTGUN THE TAILS!	60
TICKLED US PINK AWARD - MARC REW	61

OPENING CEREMONY - LET THE GAME BEGIN — 6

MAZZ & ELI'S FAVOURITE INGREDIENTS	64
TIMELESS HILL TRUFFLES	64
BOOKALAAM OLIVE GROVE	65
SUBMITTED COMPETITION RECIPE CONTENTS	66
COMPETITION RECIPE CONTENTS CONT'D	68
PICKLED DOT-TO-DOT	72
GOING DOTTY TOGETHER	74
101 BUSH CHOOKS AWARD - LIONEL 'RUFFY' RUFF	79
CITRIC FRUIT BENEFITS	82
THE GRAPES GET NIGHT SHIFT	86
BLACK PEARL PEPPERS	95
AS STUFFED AS A MARRON - JAMIE LANZINI	99
DANDELION LEAF BENEFITS	104
AFTERNOON SHENANIGANS	105
PURDY 'CRAW'FUL JOKES	106

THE COMPETITION CONTINUES

RED-CLAW KING AWARD - JUSTIN OSHEA	109
GRAPES & SALTANAS	110
LOOK INTO MY EYES - LITERALLY	112
A SHORT TRIP - WITH A LONG ENDING	115
MARRONING MELODY	117
UGH HAS AN IDEA!	122
LIPBURNER AWARD.. HANG ON WAIT?! - STOLEN	125
YABBY QUEEN AWARD - AUDREY SERDITY	127
SAMPHIRE - BEACH COOKING	129
NO MORE CRAY-Z HEAD.	137
PARTICIPATION AWARD - GAVIN ROBINSON	143
PARTICIPATION AWARD - KEVIN KNIGHT	151
ARE OUR NATURAL SPRINGS THE ANSWER?	152
THE DEHYDRATOR - DJOOL ARMY CREATOR	158
BERNIES DJAM EVIL PLAN	159
MORE OF BERNIES EVIL PLAN	160
MAZZ'S PART OF BERNIES DJAM EVIL PLAN	161
BLACK PEARL MORTICIAN SERVICE	161
BERNIE GOES OLD SCHOOL ON MAZZ	162
HERCULES COULDN'T TAKE THIS BEATING!	163
BIG BERTHA'S CRAY-Z CRAY AWARD - PAULA DAVIS	164
PARTICIPATION AWARD - ROBIN CUNNINGHAM	166
LIP BURNER AWARD - SHANTEL BERGROTH	168
PARTICIPATION AWARD - MATTHEW WILLIAMS	169
WESTERN COMMON REED - WONDER REED	172
WE'RE NOT CRAY-CIST AWARD - MARK CUZENS	173
WE'RE NOT CRAY-CIST AWARD - IAN MITCHELL	173
HUNGA DESTRUCTA AWARD - MATTHEW WILLIAMS	177
YABBIES BELONG IN THE BELLY	177
THE DUO HAVE LATE NIGHT GUESTS	179
HALF-TIME ENTERTAINMENT	181
BORN 'CRAW'LER CRAY-Z AWARD - PAUL HARFOUCHE	183
BIG RED AWARD- KANGAROO ISLAND MARRON FARM	184
ADVICE FROM THE BIG BLACK BOOT	186
EMU BERRIES - GET THEM BEFORE THEY DO!	187
PEPPY WALKING HIS PET MARRON	196

'SHELL'OCK IS ON THE CASE 192

WHERE IS OUR HEAD JUDGE?	198
ARE YOU OUR 'SHELL'OCK?	199
CRIME INVESTIGATION SLEUTH THEORY (C.I.S.T.) FORMS	264

WE RESPECT THE PEOPLE OF THE LAND — 200

BUSH BREAD VS DAMPER	202
NATIVE SEASONAL SMÖRGÅSBOARD	202
GET TO KNOW YOUR BUSH TUCKER	203
NOONGAR WORDS TO PRACTICE	203
W.R.T.P.O.T.L.	203
TRADITIONAL NOONGAR SEASONS	204

AUSSIES CRAY-Z COMPANIES — 206

BECOME A LEGEND WITH A LEGEND IN A LEGEND	206
"ALL HAIL OUR NOBLE STAR"	209
FOREST FRESH MARRON - WA	210
OLD VASSE TROUT & MARRON FARM - WA	212
KANGAROO ISLAND MARRON FARM - SA	214
YABBY DABBA DOO - NSW	216
PASES AQUA - WA	218
MERV COOPERS CRAZY CRABS - WA	220
WOODVALE FISH & LILY FARM - WA	222
MARRON GROWERS ASSOCIATION OF WA	224

RESEARCH MEMBERS — 226

BEING OVER 'BOARD?'	226
HOW 'CRAW'SOME IS YOUR LATIN?	227
ON THE HUNT FOR THE TRUE MARRON	230
PARTICIPATION AWARD - ANTHONY EDWARDS	232
'CRABBI' THE AQUA'COP'TER	234
HOW CAN YOU HELP US?	235
WELL, WELL, IT'S AN AQUIFER!	236
ROOM FOR THE WHOLE FAMILY	237
ARE THERE CRAYFISH IN OUR DRINKING WATER?	238
THE TWO TYPES OF AQUIFER	239
WHAT HAPPENS WHEN THEY STOP 'CRAW'LING?	240
SO WHO'S LOOKING AFTER WHO?	241
WHAT HAPPENS IF HERCULES WINS AGAIN?	242
IF HE TAKES WHAT HE WANTS? TO WHAT EXTENT?	242
THE CHANGE OF GROUNDWATER CONDITIONS	243
WHAT WAS KARKINOS PROTECTING?	245
NATURE CONSERVATION PARTNERS & SUPPORTERS	246
CALLING ALL CITIZEN SCIENTISTS & NATURE GURUS	247
CREEK PLAY AT E.M.P.S. - WA	248
MERCHANDISE PACKS FOR SALE	251
RESEARCH MEMBERS	252
LOG YOUR CATCH - FOR RESEARCH MEMBERS	258
RESEARCH REGISTRATION APPLICATIONS	262

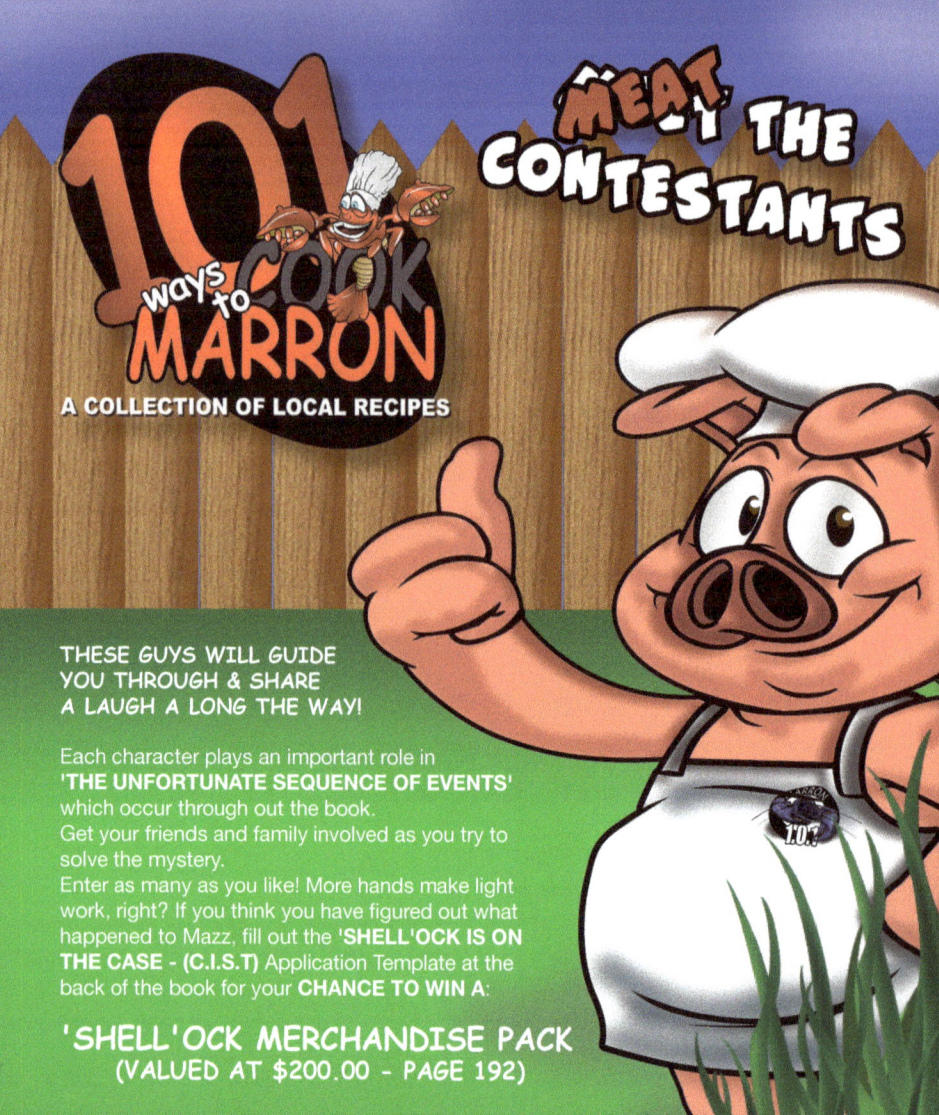

101 ways to COOK MARRON
A COLLECTION OF LOCAL RECIPES

MEAT THE CONTESTANTS

THESE GUYS WILL GUIDE YOU THROUGH & SHARE A LAUGH A LONG THE WAY!

Each character plays an important role in **'THE UNFORTUNATE SEQUENCE OF EVENTS'** which occur through out the book.
Get your friends and family involved as you try to solve the mystery.
Enter as many as you like! More hands make light work, right? If you think you have figured out what happened to Mazz, fill out the **'SHELL'OCK IS ON THE CASE - (C.I.S.T)** Application Template at the back of the book for your **CHANCE TO WIN A**:

'SHELL'OCK MERCHANDISE PACK
(VALUED AT $200.00 - PAGE 192)

CHEF MACON

The Top Chef! Chef Macon, has worked in many a pig pen across the world, including New Pork, Hong Pong, he's worked in Is'ham'ic - 'Ham'al Approved Pens and was the personal caterer for the 'Halloumi'atti for 10 years. His travels led him to Brandyburger, the locals call it Brandenburg now, but they are a 'whei'rd bunch.
When he met the locals they started chanting *"Tam exitialis est porcus cancro!"* and would not let him in the trucks carrying crayfish for superstition said that all the crays would be dead the next day!
Telling this story at the Ol' Animal Bar in Manjimup is how Chef Macon became friends with Head Chef & Judge Mazz C. Cainii. Chefs real name isn't 'Macon', it's Chris P. Bacon. He got his nickname from one of his prize dishes and his way with words.

PEPPY RINGBURNER

First off, I would just like to apologise for Peppy, Peppy's attitude is, "Good things come with a chilli on top, not a cherry." He will '**PEP**' up occasionally and put his two seeds worth in. Peppy has a tendency to always remind you about your encounter with him the next day. Peppy recruited his band members The Pearls to help with '**SPICING**' up the recipes and are going to be doing a **RED HOT CHILL PEPPER** cover for the viewers. We think his heart is in the right place, if chillies have them of course? Let's see how his half time entertainment is?

DANY D. LION

Dany's family are one of the Forefathers of medicine and **NIPCOIN** as we know it today. Many of the public have forgotten the '**LION**' Family, bar the odd '**HERB**'storian.
Dany herself, along with modern society has forgotten about her history and spends most of her time chasing her hunky crush Peppy and updating her selfies of course!.
Her tendancy of popping up in random places is unfathomable and can be quite hard to get rid of, but her passion for food shows in the coffee & salads she can help you create, which seem to out-weigh the swarms of bees & pests that consistantly come in for her nectar and the constant bee-stings that follow.

CLOVE R. LIC & K-C

Clove is a very unique bulb of garlic. Passionate about raising her children naturally and is consistantly looking for alternative to pharmacutical addictive medications. Clove will spend hours researching a topic prior to having an opinion. A very rare thing to find in the yard full of '**WEEDS**' she finds herself surrounded with.
Her bright & kind daughter K-C is always looking for an adventure. You will find her popping her head up every now and then with Eli. Clove is always walking around eating chunks of herself, as she says "If I stop everyone else getting sick, I can keep the nasty bugs away from myself too!" Her flamboyant personality is always represented by the unique ways she does her hair and the varieties of baking smells that waft through her home, make it near on impossible to keep Eli & K-C out of the fridge & pantry. She keeps us all going without even knowing.

THE CITRIC DUO - PUCKA & LIMETTA CITRON

They're not spitting, they can't stop laughing. This Citric Duo have enough zest to ruin every situation with some corny line... Some do find them quite funny and not so cringe worthy in small doses. But as Pucka the Lemon likes to say to his partner Limetta "The sweet just isn't that sweet with out the sour!"

THE GRAPES & SULTAN-A'S

These juicy morons just do not know when to stop talking! The Grapes live in tight-knit bunches, keeping an eye out for any trouble. The Black Pearls hunt the Grapes, they capture them and force them through their evil weapon '**THE DEHYDRATOR**'. This machine turns the Grapes into The Sultan-A's, mindless minions with their personalities being dried out of them, they too don't say much and are quite easy to confuse.
Look out for any signs of other victims of the Pearls.

THE BLACK PEARLS - BERNIE, UGH & BLAZE PEARL

These cute, but deadly chillies, are known as the Black Pearls. They are deviates! Always trying to swindle themselves into any situation and cause devastation.
The Head Pearl is Bernie, his bandana brother is Ugh!.. He doesn't speak much.. The third Pearl is Bernie's little nephew, Blaze who once he finds his legs you'll see his firey personality!
Keep an eye out for these guys their goal is to take over the book and run all the vegetables through their machine,
'**THE DEHYDRATOR**'
to create the Djool Army.
Wonder how they plan to do it?

THE FUN-GUYS - ANTON DE BARY & HEINRICH

These two '**FUN-GUYS**' are always trying to out-smart the other competitors. Heinrich & his brother Anton de Bary (Froogle their names), and are always looking at ways of staying ahead, regardless of the outcome. Coming in a close second in last years competition. These '**CHAMP**'ignons take to any '**SPORE**'t with caps a-blazing, As Heinrich says himself, "There ain't '**MUSH**'room in history for losers."
You can be assured that these mycologists have more up their sleeves than we give them credit for, keep an eye on them. The '**ROOMIES**' just missed out on a head judge role because there was too much debate about them being the meat of the vegetables. Besides Anton kept going around in the last competition threatening to '**CROWN**' anyone who didn't '**BUTTON**' it about his height. Let's see how they go this year?

WHAT ARE THESE BUG-GERS?

First off some of the boring stuff to help the young enthusiasts & Astacologists along the way.. All freshwater crayfish in Australia belong to the family Parastacidae. Crayfish are divided into nine groups which stem off into over 157 species. The four most common are Cherax, Euastacus, Engaewa and Astacopis. Cherax are the best known and are found all over Australia. They have quite a rapid rate of growth and have a higher tolerance to fluctuating temperatures and water conditions than some of the other species. Crayfish belong to a group of animals called Crustaceans and are part of the species category Arthropoda, a part of the Arthropod (**INSECT**) family and are known by many names depending where they are found. Western Australia has the marron, koonac & gilgie, New South Wales & Victoria share the yabby and Queensland has the red-claw. All Arthropods have a hardened outer-skeleton called cuticle (calcium carbonate which they grow by moulting (they shed their shell) exposing a soft, larger shell that hardens quickly. The crustacean are unique from the other arthropods by their two pair of antennae - an outer pair called antennae, and an inner pair called antennules. Their bodies are divided into three parts; the head, the thorax (the section that contains the legs), and the abdomen (or the tail, which is the tasty part of many large crustaceans including crayfish, prawns and lobsters). Crayfish, like many crustacean have a carapace or shield which projects backwards from the head and covers the thorax, its two functions are to protect the delicate feather-like gills. It also provides a water channel that is a constant flow of oxygenated water to pass over the gills allowing the crayfish to breathe. This means the crayfish can spend long durations of time under the water without having to surface.

YOU CAN'T MAKE THIS STUFF UP!

Crayfish are decapod crustaceans, which means they have 10 legs. These 10 include large claws called chelipeds for grasping their food, fighting and moving around. The next pair of legs consist of two small pincers for picking up food particles and stuffing them into their mouths.

But what about the ones that organise the eggs? Yes, they are called swimmerets but they don't use them for swimming as such, they are independently controlled & jointed. These are used for sorting and oxegenating their eggs on the female, so each set needs to be able to move indepenently to adjust the condition of each layer of eggs. The swimmerets also help ventilate their burrows.

Crayfish also have four independent limbs near the mouth used for directing the food. Have you ever paid attention to a crayfish mouth? Have a look next time! ;)

That counts to 20 independent limbs. **DOUBLE-DECA-POD?** Crayfish have two eyes on the end of their eyestalks but rely heavily on touch and taste, they are edible by the way.

One pair of larger antennae and their smaller antennules to feel around and help navigate the dark murky waters they call home. Many of time they have been used to help get the food from between the teeth after a meal. Surely there has to be some goodness of sucking the brains of an animal that is smart enough to operate all of those limbs whilst still figuring out how to breathe and procreate. Eastern culture must think so, they consume over 90% of the world's **'LITTLE LOBSTER'** every year.

THEIR ROLE IN THE ECOSYSTEM

Marron are classified as 'Benthic Omnivores' or Detritivorous. This means they will eat all kinds of living, dead or decaying plant and animal matter found in their habitat, including fish eggs & larvae, small invertibrates and algae, as well as juvenile or other species of crayfish.

Marron prefer parts of rivers or dams where there is a permanent source of water with wood debris and submerged leaves. They play a critical role as recyclers breaking down animal and plant matter.

As much as Marron are the largest of the Parastacidae family, they have quite a few things weighed up against them as a species. They only live in **PERMANENT WATER SOURCES** such as deep rivers and dams and are quite picky when it comes down to choosing the body of water they will reside in.

High salinity, high temperatures and oxygen in the water levels all play a vital role in keeping this species in its natural habitat. Crayfish breathe by internal gills like fish, but many (especially crayfish that burrow) can remain out of water for considerable amounts of time under humid conditions. The feather-like gills are located in chambers on each side of the body. Gill openings near the mouth help circulate oxygenated water for breathing (see diagram page 22).

Crayfish like the Koonac and Gilgie create burrows in the bank walls for the dry seasons and will stay buried underground until the water levels increase. Marron on the other hand have more of a '**GET UP AND LEAVE**' attitude and will walk great distances in search of a new home. There have been stories of convoys of marron being seen kilometres away from a water source crossing gravel roads in the middle of dry summers. Unfortunately for Marron the South-West of WA's fresh water systems are being affected by an increase in salinity and reduced water flow, which can quite regularly lead them to dying of thirst on their search for a new home.

We aren't the only ones who find marron tasty either, birds, turtles, redfin perch, trout and cobbler all enjoy crayfish in their natural diet.

They are also known for cannibalism and are always fighting for the best hiding spots or food. This often leads to one or both losing one of their Chelipeds (claws). Quite often you will find a Marron with one large and one small claw, as they can regenerate their limbs.

YABBIES SPREAD BY UNDERGROUND CREEKS

THE ONLY THING THESE GUYS DON'T DESTROY, IS MY APPETITE!

The Yabby (Cherax destructor) has the largest range of all Australian crayfish and has spread across Queensland, New South Wales, most of Victoria, South Australia and has even made its way into The Northern Territory. Being introduced into WA in the 1930's the Yabby wasted no time making itself home in the Lower South-West's riverbeds and dams. Rightfully named, its burrowing in dam and riverbank walls gave this species its name due to the damage it caused. Yabbies can tolerate long periods of drought, poor water conditions, reproduce from a young age and breeding several times a year. Making them a threat to native crayfish populations as they out-compete them in numbers for food and habitat. As Yabbies are avid breeders they can carry disease that affect our native species. It also means Yabbies are more advanced than Hairies and Smooth Marron. The spread and exploitation of Yabbies has been justified by their discovery in caves near Eneabba north of Perth. The caves have only subterranean drainage. The yabbies probably had escaped from a farm pond via the temporary surface drainage into the cave.

Of concern was the number of crayfish present; clearly a breeding population had become established, and the yabbies have undoubtedly been feeding on the native animals normally residing in the cave streams. However, a **BLIND EYE** had been turned. The caves occur in a national park, which should be off-limits to exotic fauna! Never release Yabbies into rivers and dams and they should not be used as live bait..
GOOD NEWS! They are a perfect substitute for Marron in many dishes found in this book!

HOW MANY MARRON CAN A SCOTTSMAN FIT UNDER HIS KILT?

DEPENDS ON THE SIZE OF HIS PERCH MICK!

MICK DE WIT

WHAT'S HAPPENED TO OUR LOCAL SPECIES?

Ever hear the stories from your Grandparents about the **GIANT Freshwater Crayfish?**... or of the tiny semi-transparent burrowing crayfish, with a claw that looks like it's been pumping weights with only one arm for its entire life?.. No? Well for the readers who may not have heard or for those that would love a flash-back in history. The whole lower South-West used to be home for these creatures. Hairy Marron, once the ruler of the water bodies, rivers and creeks, has now found itself in only a few small pockets. The main location being the Shannon River, **THE SHANNON NATIONAL RESERVE** and through to the back of Yeagarup. The decline in the Hairy Marron and Dil species is considered to coincide with the introduction of the Smooth Marron to the Margaret River region and the Perth Basin in the early to mid 1980's.

Both species numbers disappeared over a duration of 20 years to a point of only being found in a small parts of the lower South-West. The Hairy Marron was put under threat from the (now) more commonly placed Smooth Marron which was introduced over the **HYDRAZONE** into nearby private dams in the early 1980's (see map on next page) and quickly spread into the territories of our beloved Hairy Marron. Research was done on '**A**' section of Shannon River near **MARGERET RIVER**. Approximately 10% of marron collected were identified as hybrids, **40%** as Hairy Marron and **50%** as Smooth Marron.

The lower and middle reaches of the Margaret River have reduced habitat quality and are subject to water extraction, factors which may have influenced the ability of the Smooth Marron to replace the Mossyback. The Smooth Marron's biological invasion over the **HYDRAZONE** is the very same that we now face with the introduction of the Yabby to Western Australia over **MAN'S CREATED LINE** dividing the states.

Crayfish species are different by factors that greatly come from their environment. Is the only way to see a return of our Hairy Marron and the Burrowing Crayfish, is to be monitoring the species we find in our local regions? If you would like to help, check out the back of the book.

GEOLOGY OF THE SOUTH-WEST REGIONS

Images (opposite page) sourced from the Department of Minerals & Energy Geological Survey of Western Australia.
Geology and Hydrogeology of the Scott Coastal Plain Perth Basin.
By I. J. Baddock Record 1995/7.

Map of Tasmania sourced from: Mineral Resources Tasmania Tasmanian Geological Survey A Review of Ground Water in Tasmania.
Compiled by **C. A. Bacon** & M. Latinovic,
Record 2003/01.

THE BIGGER, THE OLDER, THE DEEPER?

Tasmania's Astacopsis gouldi or the Giant Tasmanian Crayfish is the largest crayfish in the world. Although large animals are now rare, specimens have been recorded to measure over 400mm in length with claws longer than 150mm.
They both face the same fate of extinction due to over fishing and competing with humans for land and water (above & below the ground). Have they both gone into the the depths of our fresh water aquifer flow systems?
Help us protect the locations our **CRAY-Z** natural water cleaners call home.
For more information go to page 226.

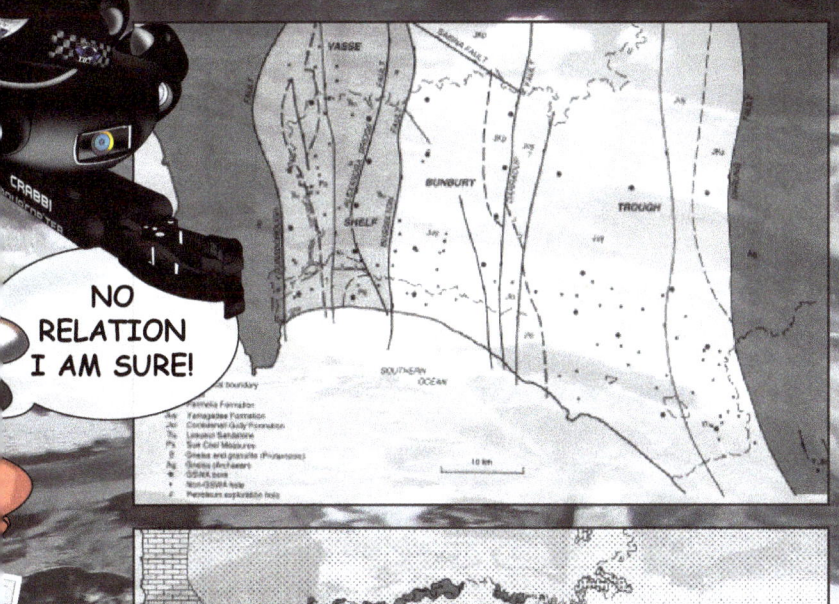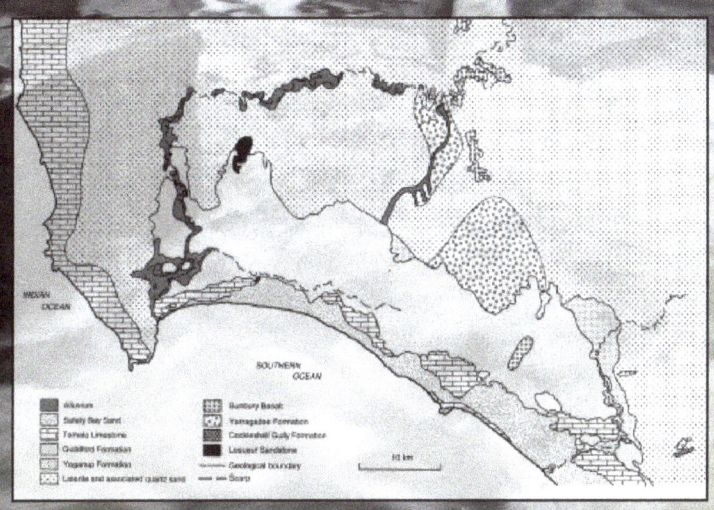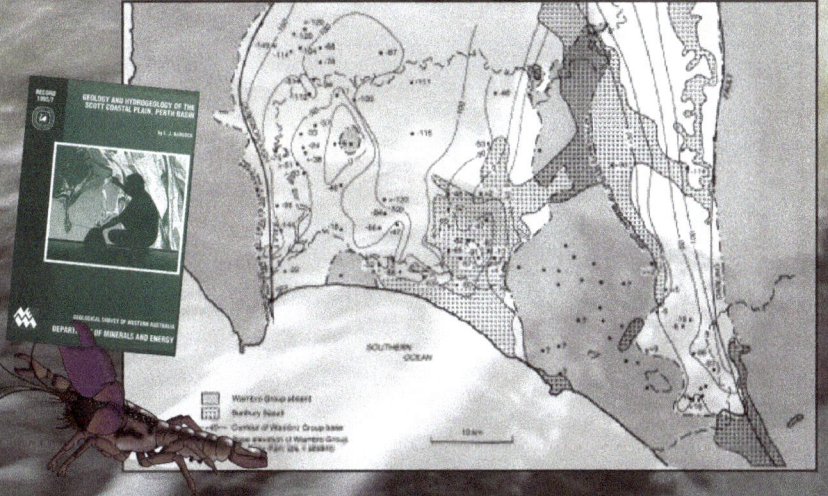

OUT COMPETED BY EARLY BREEDING CYCLES

These days it seems all we find are young, smaller sized crayfish in the local rivers & streams... and it's expected with the influx of out of season marroning and introduced species that breed nearly 20 times to our Marron breeding once! Marron reach sexual maturity at 2-3 years old whereas Yabbies can breed from 9 months and several times a year.

Marron thrive in waters 15° to 25°C and do most of their growing in the summer months when the water is warmer and will slow their growth throughout the colder months. Like most of the animals on the planet, the Marron takes full advantage of the rising temperatures of early spring and can produce between 200 & 400 eggs, the larger cows (female crayfish) can produce up to 800. During mating, males produce a packet of sperm the females will use to fertilise their eggs. Once fertilised, the females carry the eggs under their tail, This is called the **'BERRIED'** state until the eggs hatch. For a few months the larvae cling to the thousands of hairs under their mums tail, moulting their shells and feeding from their mother.

The waterways are no place for the tiny shrimp-like crustaceans, so staying close to their mother when they drop off from under her tail in early spring plays a vital role in the survival for these little ones, expecially since they are vulnerable to cannibalism by other marron and other crayfish species.

AN INTRODUCTION TO MARRON

OUT COMPETED BY EARLY BREEDING CYCLES

This chart represents how many fertilized eggs each individual yabby can produce over the 36 month period it takes for marron to reach a mature age of fertility. By the time a marron has bred for the first time (producing 400 eggs), a yabby has matured at nine months and has bred several times a year (producing an average 300 eggs each time). Sounds to me like the rabbits are getting a bit of '**RUFF JUSTICE**' on this one.

WHAT IS UNDER THAT HARD SHELL?

The crayfish has a carapace or a shield that starts from the head and covers the entire thorax. Aside from protecting the gills, it also allows for the constant flow of oxygenated water over the gills so the crayfish can breathe on land as well as in water above & below the sedimentary layer..

WHAT DO I HAVE IN MY NET?

How many people do you know that think they can tell the marron from a yabby? or male from female? **WHICH IS MALE BELOW?** Well I can tell you, majority of them would be incorrect and quite regularly could find that they in fact have a large yabby instead... It can be quite hard at the best of times let alone at night on the side of a river looking at one or a small handful of crayfish in your net.

The wrong assumption can cost you up to $50,000 or even jail time outside of restricted season dates on crayfish in your area.

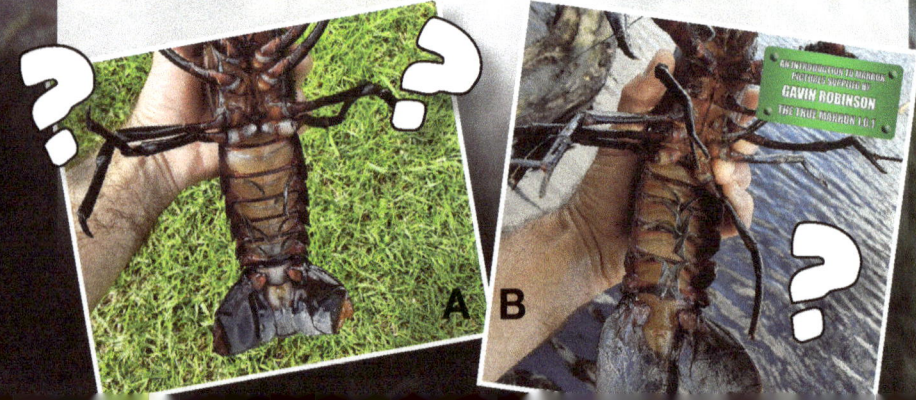

WHAT SEX IS MY CRAYFISH?

When catching or purchasing your crayfish for your tank, it is important to check the sex: Firstly if catching Marron, you must throw back **ALL FEMALES** to help the regeneration of the species and when preparing your tank you want to keep two males to four females (purchase these from a supplier so you have a reciept of purchase), this limits fights and your crayfish becoming injured in territorial contests. The best way to tell is to flip the crayfish over and look at the base of their legs. No one likes to bare their bits and if done incorrectly crayfish will try and nip you with their claws (Chelipeds).

FEMALE (COW)
Gonopores: First segment - Second Leg
Promanant opening base of sternum.
Shorter & more feathered swimmerets.

AN INTRODUCTON TO MARRON

HAIRY MARRON - MOSSYBACK (CHERAX TENUIMANUS)

Hairy Marron or Mossybacks as they are known to the region for their distinct hair-like tufts on their shell. These monsters can grow to more than 450 mm in total length. They are one of the largest freshwater crayfish species in the world with specimens having been recorded in excess of 2kg! Hairies were predominantly found in the **ALBANY-FRASER OROGEN** and stretched across the lower part of the Perth basin, prior to the smooth marron being introduced into nearby private dams and quickly spread. This led to interbreeding with our local Mossyback species. While adults are readily identified from the Smooth Marron (Cherax cainii), hybrids do occur and are more difficult to identify. Good thing to look for is the thickness of the claw. Hairy Marron have a narrow cheliped and have very prominent swimmerets and did I mention they are **HAIRY?**

MALE OR FEMALE, ALWAYS PUT A HAIRY MARRON BACK!
and report the location either in the:
RESEARCH MEMBERS LOG YOUR FIND Section, page 254.
Or by contacting Margaret River Nature Conservation Centre, page 247.

SMOOTH MARRON (CHERAX CAINII)

The restaurant favourite! Growing to dinner plate size, the Smooth Marron were introduced into the natural habitat of the Hairy Marron in the early to mid 1980s and are currently found at all known population sites for the Hairy Marron.

With their thicker claws and smooth body appearance these lip-smackers won the attention of the French and other overseas restaurants quite quickly, leaving very little availability to the general public unless purchased at a restaurant, Marron season only lasts from 1-2 weeks with limited bagging numbers.

The Smooth Marron love permanent water sources and have been found walking across gravel roads out in the middle of nowhere making their way to the next water body as if by some sixth sense. Stories have been told of 40 marron walking neatly single file through dry, gravel rock areas of the South-West, thanks to the water bladder the marron have under their carapace (see page 22).

KOONAC (CHERAX PREISSII & CHERAX GLABER)

The widespread Koonac, Cherax preissii (Moore River to just east of Albany) & the Restricted Koonac, Cherax glaber (Dunsborough to Windy Harbour), up to 250mm in length. Koonacs can be seen as the marron's heavyweight (but smaller) relative. Their chelipeds are quite large and robust. They are serated on the inside with quite a prominent nub on the inside of each claw, being pinched by one of these would leave an imprint in any child's memory for the remainder of their lives (personal memory). These crays spend times of drought burrowed into the mud & will stay there for months at a time waiting for the next downpour.

Koonacs heads have four keels, two standing more prominent than the other two. With no spines or bumps on their carapace and telson, it gives the Koonac a 'sleek-black bullet' look that can make it easly mistaken for a large yabby. These beasts have ruled the creeks of W.A. well before the introduction of Yabbys in 1932.

GILGIE (CHERAX QUINQUECARINATUS & CHERAX CRASSIMANUS)

The widespread Gilgie, Cherax quinquecarinatus (Moore River to just east of Albany), the Restricted Gilgie, Cherax crassimanus (Margaret River to Denmark region). Gilgies are the cleaners of most streams, rivers and irrigation dams throughout the South-West and can sometimes find themselves at the bottom of your marron net or in that empty Coke can at the edge of the road in the water run-offs. Gilgies burrow into the bank walls thoughout droughts and are very versatile to the riverways and washouts it calls home.

As kids, most people of the region will have stories of going down to the creek at the bottom of the street and moving a few rocks in search of these little ones. Gilgies quite normally get mistaken for baby marron, but are in fact, are very different.. Gilgies also have five keels on their heads like marron, but only two pairs of spines on their rostrum.

Another great way to tell them apart is the claws, Smooth Marron claws are wider and the Gilgie have very distinct speckles on their claws. An adult Gilgie can only reach up to 130mm, just longer than a bankcard.

DIL / FRESHWATER BURROWING CRAYFISH

These little bug-gers are very hard to find and not very well known of, at full size they grow to only 5cm with a semi-translucent carapace, purple claws and a reddish tail. One of the most distinctive features of the Burrowing Crayfish species is its one large claw that makes it look like a one handed arm wrestler. It uses its claw to burrow into the river bank and to get through the vegetated tributaries of each of their areas, where they search for any dead decaying plant and organic matter they need to eat.
As mentioned earlier in the book, the Burrowing Crayfish Engaewa species are **ALL CRITICALLY ENDANGERED** and the swampy headwater creek habitats where they live; Margaret River, Walpole and Dunsborough, being substantially altered by clearing of native vegetation, cattle grazing, draining, afforestation practices and **'POND'SY SCHEMES.**
Now, with little funding to protect these mini mud-bugs, sadly the Burrowing Crayfish of either species is a rare find indeed!

PROBABLY WOULD OF 'HERD' OF ME IF I WAS A CHERAX!

ENGAEWA PSEUDOREDUCTA
ENGAEWA WALPOLEA
ENGAEWA REDUCTA

AN INTRODUCTION TO MARRON

YABBY (CHERAX DESTRUCTOR)

Yabbies are an introduced species to WA. Originally native to New South Wales, Victoria and South Australia, they were stocked into farm dams in WA in 1932. Yabbies can now be found in some of the south-west rivers and dams.

Unlike Marron their heads have four keels, two being more prominent and no spines on the rostrum. The inner edges of the claws have a layer of obvious hairs not found on other crayfish species native to WA.

As much as Yabbies are smaller than Marron they make up for it in numbers (page 21). They are fast breeders and their name '**DESTRUCTOR**' says it all, rightfully named by Ellen Clark in 1936, these crayfish are highly territorial and aggressive towards pretty well anything they come across. They destroy riverweed crops and natural vegetation is quickly demolished, due to the vast numbers this species can generate in a just a few years.

The Yabby is very popular in pet shops for its durability to water quality levels and ease of breeding.

'POLYPS' IT'S A GASTROLITH

While talking to Justin from Old Vasse Trout & Marron Farm. He showed me these jars with white looking stones found on the banks of his marron dams. Upon doing research I found that they are actually from the heads of freshwater crayfish. These have an appearance of a hardened button mushroom and are called **'GASTROLITHS'** in latin it breaks down to mean: Gastro = Stomach & Lith = Stone. Personally I believe they should be named **'CALCI-LITHS'** as they are quite literally little calcium deposits used to help create the crayfish exoskeleton during moulting. T.H. Huxley in his book called The Crayfish published in 1880, calls them **'BRAIN STONES'** at least he was looking at it rationally.

So what's the process that is under so much debate on what is it called? Perhaps it might give us come answers.

The process is quite amazing, once the crayfish reaches its moulting period the horhomes that drive the process to extract calcium carbonate from the exoskeleton form the excess as these little calcium stones. Only freshwater crayfish form these 'Calciliths,' unlike their salt water cousins who live in calcium rich saltwater which makes these unique to freshwater species of crays. After the crayfish has moulted, the 'Calciliths'.. sorry, I know! That was quick! I can't call them **STOMACH STONES** or gastroliths, every species on the planet can have those and Calciliths are not used to break down unprocessed foods and are not swallowed rocks to assist with a lack of teeth..

So! The **'CALCILITHS '** are reabsorbed and used in the strengthening of the new exoskeleton to help it protect itself from predators. If you are lucky enough to have watched the moulting process of a crayfish, you will notice how the crayfish will eat its old shell to absorb the very last nutrients it needs to strengthen its armour faster. The larger the crayfish, the more calcium carbonate is needed to strengthen the shell. This could be why crayfish show signs of aggression to others of the same and other species prior to the moulting period as the hormones start, the cravings for calcium kicks in. Sounds similar to people and our milk cravings. The people of the land around the world have been found with necklaces made of these unique Calciliths & Gastroliths from other species creating spectacular jewelry and were even used in dentistry to fill holes in teeth. No one is sticking stomach stones in their mouth as a fake tooth. Much like people require calcium for strong and healthy bones, so does a freshwater crayfish to maintain its armour. They cannot get it from the waters it calls home, unlike their salt water

cousins. Gastroliths and '**CALCILITHS**' have been used in traditional medicine for their absorbent and antacid properties for a large range of different conditions & diseases including: the plague, a cure for syphilis, the assistance with breaking down bladder stones, 'Calciliths assist with stomach problems (including stomach ulcers & the breaking down of stomach stones **A.K.A** Gastroliths. Seems fitting to give these '**CALCI-LITHS**' the recognition they deserve.
Jump online to check out:

THE TRUE MARRON 1.0.1's
EATEN OR SMOKED SAME BENEFITS
The Black Pearls have held our office hostage and have our workers all grinding down the Calci-Liths into powder and putting it into gelatin capsules.
All Calci-Liths are cleaned and processed prior to being ground into powder form.
(I should know! They are making me do it!)
No added ingredients though.
(they don't want to hurt you, just win the competition).

100% GROUND CALCIUM CARBONATE
100% HIDE VEGETARIAN CAPSULES
100% VEGETARIAN DERIVED FROM HPMC
Pure natural plant fiber, care for your health
Irritant-free and Preservative-free
CAPSULES SIZES: 1 ONLY
www.thetruemarron101.au/SAMEBENEFITS
www.thetruemarron101.au/TINCTURKING

BLACK PEARL
MORTICIAN SERVICE

REST IN POWDER.

D.J.A.M. SHREDDER WASTE
**CRAYFISH
CALCI-LITH**
ONE CAPSULE EVERY 2 DAYS
NATURAL CRAYFISH
CALCIUM CARBONATE

TA*S*_EST_

AN INTRODUCTION TO MARRON

GEEZ! WAIT FOR ME! I'M A DIL NOT DULL!

TIME UP EVER

AN INTRODUCTON TO MARRON

WE'RE NOT **THE TRUE MARRON** **1.0.1** **CRAYFISCIST**

WOODVALE FISH & LILY FARM - CALINDA ANDERSON

Calinda owns and runs the Woodvale Fish and Lily Farm. She has benefited from her family's long experience in this field and now together with her team of experienced staff they can confidently assist with all types of water gardening. When asked about what her aim is for her business, she said "My hope is that everyone that comes to the Woodvale Fish and Lily Farm enjoys the experience, walking through the gardens and ponds, enjoying the fish, the vegetable gardens, even visiting the chickens, inspiring people to have a pond, fish or aquaponics and to do it naturally with no chemicals". Calinda makes regular appearances on Channel 9 The Garden Gurus, you can see many of her videos on water gardening in the library section on her website;

**www.woodvalefishandlilyfarm.com.au,
Youtube or at www.thegardengurus.tv.**

THE WOODVALE FISH & LILY FARM TEAM

If you have any interest at all in ponds, water lilies, water plants, aquaponics, edible fish, Koi or Goldfish then you have to visit The Woodvale Fish and Lily Farm.

The Woodvale Fish and Lily Farm is arguably one of Australia's best Water Garden Nurseries, with over 100 ponds on display showcasing and selling 50 varieties of Water Lilies, (including Hardy, Tropical, Miniature and Night Flowering Lilies), along with a large selection of water plants, 1000's of Koi and Goldfish, native Fish, Silver Perch, Rainbow Trout, Barramundi, Marron and Yabbies.

The Woodvale Fish and Lily Farm stock everything you will need to set up and filter a pond or an aquaponics system. They carry a large range of pumps, pre-formed ponds, pond liner, filter options, gravels, water plant potting mix, fish food of all kinds, and pond lighting.

The Woodvale Fish & Lily Farm freely offers advice and information on how to set up and filter ponds and we recommend and use environmentally friendly, natural, non-chemical solutions.

Established 20 years ago, and with many years of experience, the Woodvale Fish and Lily Farm are widely considered the experts on Natural Water Gardening. You will see their articles featuring regularly with the Garden Guru's Magazine and TV show, Greenfingers TV show and Newspapers.

SURRENDER UNWANTED FISH

Not only is it illegal, it is really important that you don't release any unwanted fish into the waterways.

If you have any unwanted cold water fish that need a new home, and you can't find anyone to take them, you can surrender them here to Woodvale at anytime that we are open.

And sorry we don't pay for any surrendered fish, we only purchase from licensed breeders.

GO TO OUR WEBSITE FOR MORE INFORMATION.

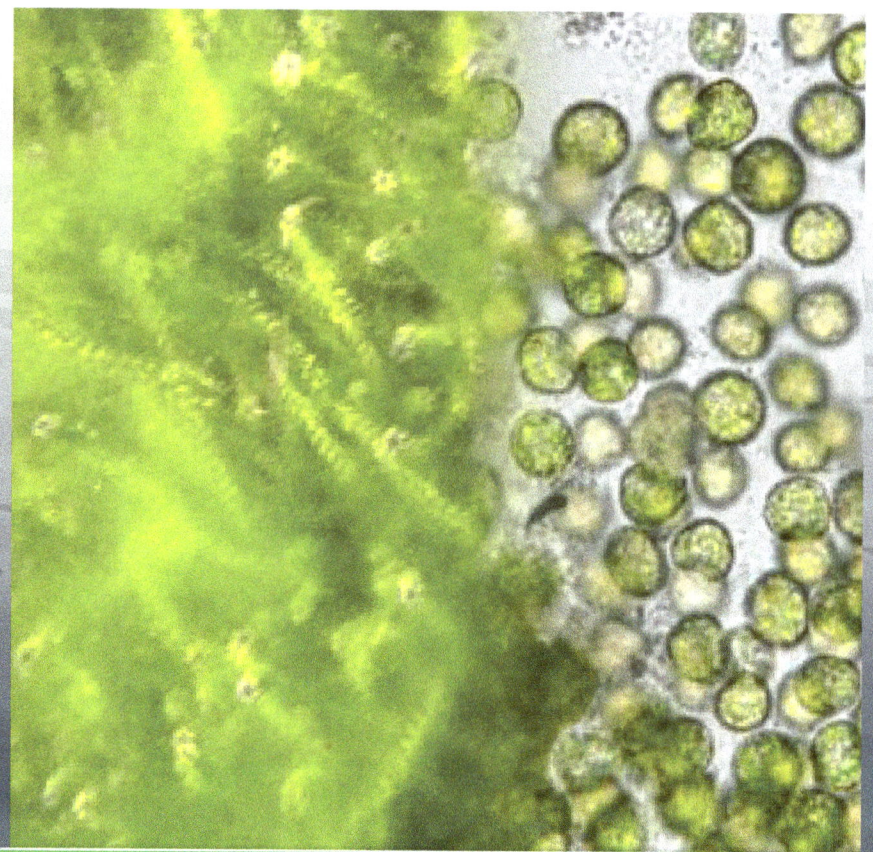

ALGAE, WHAT'S IT ALL ABOUT?

Algae is not harmful, so don't panic, it is a natural food source, a fish breeding ground, a shelter and provides a good place for baby fish and tadpoles to start their new lives. In fact fish are generally happier in green water, but visually it is unattractive to us, we want to see the clear water.

Algae is a primitive plant that is exclusively aquatic, plant size can range from microscopic to large filamentous strands, colour can vary from brown/green through to bright green, texture can range from slimy to quite a dry feeling.

Algae will grow in nearly any body of water, you can place a bucket of fresh water in a sunny spot and over time algae will grow. Filamentous algae is seasonal and will general grow more rapidly in spring and at the end of summer.

Single celled or green water algae can be present at any time, this generally occurs in new ponds during the first 4-6 weeks, when filters are cleaned out too often and ponds with no or incorrect filtration.

WE REWARD YOU FOR GIVING YOUR CRAY THE BEST!

Below is the best growth food available for Crustaceans (ie Marron, Yabbies, Koonacs). All fish food is packaged in store in to 2lt jars and 5lt buckets. These containers include a $2 deposit, which is refunded when returned empty. You can order online to collect in store, or we can post anywhere in Australia. If not collecting in store you might prefer to choose from our economical Australia-wide post packs.
If you can't make it to our store we can post or courier any fish food Australia-wide, from 3kg – 20kg.

AN INTRODUCTON TO MARRON

HOW MUCH TO FEED YOU ASK?

his depends on what is naturally occuring in the enviroment that they are living in, as they will eat algae etc, Generally we say, 1 pellet per animal per day - try feeding in the same spot and don't add more pellets until you can see that they have eaten it all.

WE ALL PLAY OUR PART IN PROTECTING THE ENVIROMENT. JUST LIKE THESE GUYS!
WOODVALEFISHANDLILYFARM.COM.AU

WHAT ELSE CAN I FEED MY CRAY?

Crayfish are principally vegetarian and will survive well on a diet of waterweed and almost any thinly cut vegetables such as pumpkin, potato, celery (including leaves), apples, cabbage leaves, zucchini medallions, or shelled peas and other fruits. You can also give them small amounts of meat or fish but it is not necessary. Crayfish need to have a sinking pellet food as a staple. Sinking shrimp pellets are perfect. They also like to eat vegetables as well as any decaying matter. Since fish eat shrimp pellets too, make sure you drop enough of the pellets around the crayfish's hiding place so that they can get to them. They may also eat some regular fish food flakes if they make it their way, but this is not enough for them.

The important point to remember is not to overfeed crayfish. Crayfish only have a small stomach and will stop eating when full, leaving the remainder of the food. They do not need to be fed every day. A good feeding schedule would be one to two small pieces of food every two to three days. Remember to remove any left-over food after two hours. They can also eat some frozen foods, such as daphnia, blood worms, frozen fish, and brine shrimp. Cooked chicken can also make for a great occasional treat.

AVOID using cat food or any canned fish products. Canned fish is high in salt and preservatives and is actually more expensive than a three dollar container of shrimp pellets that would last a single crayfish more than a year. If you are going to get a pet, take the effort to take care of it properly by feeding it what it needs, **NOT CAT FOOD.**

> BE 'SHORE' TO KEEP THINGS OFF THE EDGES, I LIKE TO WONDER A'BOOT'

A PART OF THE FAMILY

A few of the crayfish I had in a 8000ltr swimming pool in the family shed. To see the joy on my kid's faces as they watched the crays mingle with the 30cm trout and 20cm goldfish. Often in summer it was the perfect temperature to get in there ourselves and let the fish swim between our legs. A perfect way to teach the kids about our native freshwater ecosystem. - Adam T. Purdy

A GOOD WATER FLOW HELPS KEEP THE PARASITES OFF OUR BACKS

KEEPING CRAYFISH

101 WAYS TO COOK MARRON
PARTICIPATION AWARD
IAN MITCHELL
THE TRUE MARRON 1.0.1

GET THE RIGHT TANK FOR YOUR CRAYFISH

Like most creatures, you will find each crayfish will have its own personality and can be quite mesmerising to watch as they mingle and declare ownership of their area.

The only species sold as pets are the Dam Yabby, the Marron & the Red Claw. These are hardy species that require little maintenance and will live from two-five years in captivity.

When you are transporting the crayfish, say via car, truck, or bus, be sure not to move it around too much. This could result in what some people call '**CRAYFISH SOUP**'. This may sound funny, but it is a serious term that can cause your crayfish to become over stressed and extremely confused.

To set up an aquarium for crayfish you need a good aeration system, gravel (preferably enough for them to dig burrows in), some small pebbles and some large hollow or cavernous rocks which the crayfish can hide in during the day.

Crayfish like to organise their surroundings, so don't put anything in the tank you don't want moved around or eaten. Water weeds are a favourite of all crayfish and help with water maintenance as well. Our suggestion is to grow your own water weeds in a separate tank to keep up a constant supply.

They need a tank with a pH of 7.0 (neutral) that has a temperature between 21–24°C. One crayfish needs at least 17– 40L or 40cm2 of water all to themselves.

Crayfish like a current flow, that allows them to sit and have the food come to them. Top flow filters work well at circulating the water. Don't use an undergravel filter. Crayfish like to dig, which can jam the filter. Try and stay away from using sand in the tank. Crays like to dig and will stir up the dirt which will block the filter over time. Use small rocks and gravel as the crays will re-arrange and construct their own shelters, If creating tunnels and caves for your crayfish, remember to allow entry from both sides.

This will stop any fish getting cornered and eaten by the cray. Crayfish love the dark so remember;

THE BRIGHT PRETTY AQUARIUMS LIGHTS ARE FOR YOU!

FROM HARDCASE TO ABSOLUTE SOFTY

Crayfish in captivity typically live only about 2-3 years, but with proper treatment they can live to 7-8 years.

Crayfish that are old will feed at night and the younger ones feed during the day.

Crayfish outgrow their exoskeleton from time to time and shed it in a process called '**MOULTING**'. Crayfish, like all arthropods shed or moult their outer skin in order to grow. This happens every three to four weeks in small crayfish (4-5 cm). The length of time between each moult increases as the animal get older to once a year in full grown animals. Most Cherax species take about one and half years to reach maturity (15-20 cm). During the moulting phase the crayfish will stop eating and reduce activity, until on the day of the moult it will appear motionless. Crayfish moult their shell (ecdysis) by splitting their tail along the back and then flicking the old shell off. The head and claws are removed last. Once the shell is removed, crayfish are very soft and will hide until they have expanded into their new shell and the shell has hardened. It is advisable to leave the old shell in the tank as the crayfish will eat it as a source of calcium. Adding a small amount of calcium carbonate to the water will help make a stronger shell. When crayfish shed their exoskeleton, they are extremely vulnerable and will look for a place to hide. Provide plenty of cover and remove all predatory creatures (including large snails and aggressive fish). Some people even place their crayfish in a separate tank to protect it while it is moulting.

Do not handle your crayfish until a new exoskeleton is fully developed (about one week). Crayfish love to explore new territory and are great at escaping, so make sure you have protected any openings in the filter and have kept the lid firmly placed on the tank. If a crayfish escapes, it can dehydrate and die in just a few hours, so it's very important to be vigilant about this.

AHEM! MOVE ALONG! NOTHING TO SEE HERE!

DR. DULANA HERATH & PASES AQUA - WA

Dr. Dulana Herath, a passionate biologist with a lifelong interest in water, ornamental/ native fish and natural ecosystems founded the company in 2013. The company was initially named Perth Aquatic, Seed and Ecological Services Pty Ltd, and in 2017 split into two sister businesses PASES Aqua and PASES Eco.

Blue marron crayfish is a low-maintenance native pet and demand is going 'through the roof' worldwide.

Dr. Dulana Herath from PASES Aqua Pty Ltd had a chat with ABC news regarding the increasing demand for Electric Blue Marron to keep as pets. "They won't fetch the newspaper or cuddle you on the couch at the end of a long day, but pet owners are shelling out record dollars for ornamental blue marron during the **COVID-19** pandemic." Explained Dr. Herath "Blue marron is becoming increasingly popular as an ornamental pet and can sell for up to $250." Producers say they are receiving more enquiries than ever during the **COVID-19** pandemic about the spider-like freshwater crayfish. Industry estimates just 1 tonne of the rare electric blue crustacean is produced in WA each year.

The freshwater crayfish species can range in colour from jet-black to brown, striped and red, but it is cobalt blue marron that is becoming increasingly popular as showpieces in aquariums across Australia and the world.

"Blue marron is quite rare, so the prices we fetch are generally double if not triple the price of a standard black marron".

"It's even treated differently from black marron, even in the export documentation, where there's a different set of rules if you're exporting for the aquarium trade as opposed to the food industry."

AN 'INTERACTIVE' PET FOR ALL AGES

Dulana Herath is an aquatic biologist who also sells blue marron in the domestic market and says a fully grown female can sell for up to $250, depending on its size.

"There is huge demand. We get emails just about every day and there's just not enough producers of blue marron," he said.

"We've had inquiries from all over the world during the pandemic, including from the US, Europe and China." Mr Herath says blue marron is considered lucky in some South-East Asian countries, which is driving demand, but there is also increased interest from within WA. "Marron are pretty attractive, they move like spiders and they're very interactive," he said. "And because it's a WA native a lot of people locally are trying them as pets."

This article was originally featured on www.abc.net.au.

CHECK OUT THEIR FULL RANGE OF FINGERLINGS TOO!

PASES AQUA

WWW.PASESAQUA.COM.AU

No: 2/9 Merino Entrance,
Cockburn Central
6164, Western Australia

RULER OF THE TANK - RULER OF THE UNDERWORLD

Keep your crayfish safe from other fish. Your crayfish can live in a tank with other fish, as long as you don't have any bottom dwellers, because crayfish like to clean the bottom of your tank.
If you have any pricy or just special fish in your tank, then you may think twice about adding a crayfish to the mix. They are not just bottom dwellers, but are also scavengers and hunters, which means that they will swipe at passing fish, though this is mostly just amusing to watch and they rarely are able to attack fish. Mostly, the crayfish attack fish that are getting sick and sinking toward the bottom of the tank. They'll stay away from strong, healthy fish.
If you have large or aggressive fish, then there's a chance they can go after your crayfish too. Goldfish, trout and crayfish tend to get along in large open areas.

A GRAMMATICAL ERROR IN TRANSLATIONS OVER TIME?

GREEK (25 BC - 50 AD)
Carcinus is a giant crayfish in Greek mythology that inhabited the lagoon of Lerna. He is a secondary character in the myth of the twelve labors of Heracles (Heracles, Greek divine being), On Hera's orders (the Goddess of Marriage), Carcinus attacks Hercules while he fought the Hydra of Lerna (serpentine water monster). As a reward to the crayfish for his actions, Hera (the Full Moon) turns him into the constellation of Cancer that is represented in our star signs today.

GREEK (25 BC - 50 AD)
Translated 'karkinos' the Latin word for crab or crayfish into cancer. The name applied to various diseases now distinguished, including an ulcerating sore & malignant tumor in medicine ie: a cancer.

WESTERN SOCIETY: (2002 - 2022 AD)
Religion shuns the shellfish for being a scavenger, Yet it is classified as a gourmet food? Cancer is a taboo word.. Shhh! Even saying the word can cause you to quieten a room! Say the word **CRABS**! and people clear the room like a grenade was just thrown on the floor. Oh! How time flies!.. and they think we are **CRAY-Z!**

Meanwhile, Cancer is the only sign ruled by the moon. All crayfish river or sea, share a special connection to the orbitals cosmic body.

Ironically the crayfish '**RISES WITH THE MOON**' and the health benefits of crayfish are all known to help with the treatment of cancer. It stimulates your inner life whilst giving you energy and endorphins too, sort of like a magnetic recharge.
Either way the connection our world-wide mud-bugs have with the Universe is unlike any other species on the planet (See '**POLYPS**' It's a Gastrolith page 32). I think there may of been a smudge on the paper in translation when the stories where told of the battle between the Hydra (serpent symbol used by medicine), the crayfish (protector or disease bringer?) and Hercules (protector of mankind).

PSEUDO-HYGINUS, ASTRONOMICA 2. 23
(trans. Grant) (Roman mythographer 2nd A.D.) '**CANCER**'.
The Crab is said to have been put among the stars by the favour of Juno (Hera), because, when Hercules had stood firm against the Lernaean Hydra, the crab had snapped at his foot from the swamp (could it of been an Astacus astacus?). Hercules, enraged at this, had killed it, Juno (Hera) put it among the constellations to acknowledge the crayfish's selfless service and bravery."
If you see crayfish in your dreams, see it as a reflection of the selfless deeds you may have done or are about to do for others. Not a reason to make an uncomfortable Doctors appointment.

MEAT MAZZ - OUR HEAD JUDGE

Mazz is the mastermind behind a heap of the recipes you see inside this book. He has spent years and years licking screens, recipe books and billboards to give you guys, what he calls his '101 ways to **COOK US**'. He said "Personally, I felt I was the only one good enough to teach you how we like to be handled." Can't really argue can we?

"I have travelled all over Australia seeing how my native cousins like to be cooked. The Eastern staters aren't getting half the attention they would like.. the humans seem more focussed on a '**FLAT-HEADED**' Bug, some guy called Moreton."

"My mate Murray (Spiny to his friends) does really well, he has visitors that come flocking to his favourite hangouts, 8 months of the year. Mazz has been looking at ways of increasing his own popularity not just in restaurants but in the family home too."

"It is great to see the restaurants supplying recipes as well, but the main style I am looking for is seeing who can bring the marron into the home and make it a family meal. Other key points are simplicity, and impact of flavour" Mazz added.

"With the line up of judges chosen, the competitors really have their claws & limbs full having to impress these sets of taste buds."

'MEAT THE JUDGES

MEAT ALUNIO - MAZZ'S ~~MUSCLE~~ MUSSEL

"**ALLO**! I am Alunio Carteri from the West. My family once lived in great abundance! We are the only large bivalve here and some of my family can grow over 100mm, but most of us only get to 40-80mm. But over the last 50 years our family has been at war with the **BIG BLACK BOOT**.

We made home in the slower flowing waters, where conditions were right enough for us to burrow for safety. We would bury ourselves a few inches into the sediments, keeping ourselves hidden from predators. We would just have our shell showing to allow us to filter-feed on the light current. Times were tough, I lost my Family and my Chicka to a metal cage that dragged along the river floor releasing them from their hiding places. The screams were horrific! By the time the dirt had settled, they were gone..

From that day on, I! Alunio Carteri! declared to find the **BIG BLACK BOOT** from above and that one day! One Day! I will face him and '**HE**' will see just how bad of a mussell I am! I will not wash! I will not be **PURGED!** He will remember me for life! Do not laugh! I am big enough to pack a punch!

But anyway!.. *cough *cough (clearing throat)

I feel like I've been slurping on a dusty old vacuum cleaner. the **BIG BLACK BOOT** is back stirring up the river banks! I'm sure you can understand why I am cranky? They have no respect at all!

Sorry about that.. I get a little carried away."

'MEAT' THE JUDGES

"WHERE WAS I? AH! YES!"

"It is a pleasure to be meeting you! Let me tell you about my kind and how we can make your camping trip a real winner or a real doozy!

Next time you are out camping and want to add a little style to your dinner, go for a walk along the near-by creek or waterway and see if you can find some of us hidden among the creek bed. We are normally black to a dark brown with reddish tinge. Most of the time, we will have a thin layer of algae growing on our shell. If you are lucky enough to find some of us, please do not go overboard, our numbers are hard to replace due to our weird breeding style (once fertilized our larvae hitch a ride on a fish, or they won't survive.)

Give us a good wash to get off any algae and dirt residue, then stick us in a bucket of **CLEAN, FRESH WATER** to allow our bodies time to get rid of any nasty contaminants that could seriously make you or the one you are trying to impress, really sick! When purged correctly, we can bring life to any meal, expecially ones with the stars as candles.

There are a few recipes I have put in. If you are nice and treat us well, we won't make you sick."

'MEAT' THE JUDGES

MEAT COBBA! - NOT A CAT-FISH!

"I'm Cobba! Real name is Tandanus Bostocki, but everyone kept making 'bum jokes'. So Cobba it is!

Mazz thought it to be a good idea if I took some time to tell you about myself and how to handle me if you ever come across me in the rivers and are looking for a good feed.

So, let me start with how to identify myself! I'm a Mottled Brown Cobbler, I am the only native cobbler and the largest freshwater fish in the South-West. I may look a little weird, but let me tell you! I taste really good! You don't find many of us around as much anymore. Trout are prettier and the younger one will normally bite thoughout the day and dusk before the larger ones join us on the Night Patrol. First off it's good to point out my eel like tail. This makes me different from most other catfish species. My colour is normally a darkish-brown, but if I am in clear water my colour will get lighter to help me hide. Check out the Barbels surrounding my mouth! I don't like the word '**WHISKERS**', I'm not a **CAT**-Fish!

One thing you really need to look out for though, are my spikes on my first dorsal fin and both my pectoral fins. They are armed with glands that release a very painful venom. I really am sorry for any injuries you may get. We don't purposefully seek you out to harm you, it is to stop predators from eating us."

"A good trick if you have been '**STABBED**' by one of our spikes, is to place the stung body part '**IN HOT WATER.**' without burning the skin of course! (I'd suggest 50°C) The warm water helps break down the venom.

'**DO NOT USE ICE!**' This will actually make the pain worse!. After immersing the area in the hot water, you will still need to seek medical attention if the pain persists.

On the bright side, I am quite nocturnal so it is quite rare for anyone to see me. It's not that I am anti-social, I just don't like hurting people. I usually wait until all my neighbours are asleep before heading out to find a feed for myself. My diet consists of '**BAD**' marron and other crayfish (Not Mazz though, he is my friend), molluscs and small invertebrates.

Most of my family are quite muscly fish, which is really good for you as it means a good fight if you happen to catch us and nice, soft, delicate fillets after that long day hike.

I have submitted a few recipes for you to try.

Please let me know what you think! They are old family secrets!"

'MEAT' THE JUDGES

TANDANUS BOSTOCKI

HI! I'M TROUDY! YOU CAN FIND OUT WHERE TO CATCH ME ON PAGE 208

PREPARING YOUR MARRON

PREPARING YOUR CRAYFISH
PICTURE SUPPLIED BY
MATTHEW WILLIAMS
THE TRUE MARRON 4 U

PREPARING YOUR CRAYFISH

With all crayfish you should always remember to put them in clean water (purge) and let them flush out any traces of mud in their system before cooking.
Crayfish as scavengers will eat anything that they find in their river, stream or dam. Due to agriculture chemical run offs, worms and other diseases that can affect the meat and '**CONTROLLED**' Marron numbers, many people prefer purchasing their marron from known breeders. We have included **A FEW COMPANIES THAT SUPPLY TO THE GENERAL PUBLIC** at the back of the book for you (page 206-215)
WHO ALL DO THE PURGING FOR YOU! GO CRAY-Z!

HOW DO YOU COOK A CRAYFISH?

TO BOIL: Keep the cray in salted boiling water for about 10-12 minutes or until their shells turn a bright orange colour. Put in cold water immediately afterwards to stop the cooking process.

TO GRILL: Cut the cray in half lengthwise, baste with a mild marinade and grill flesh-side up until flesh turns opaque white.

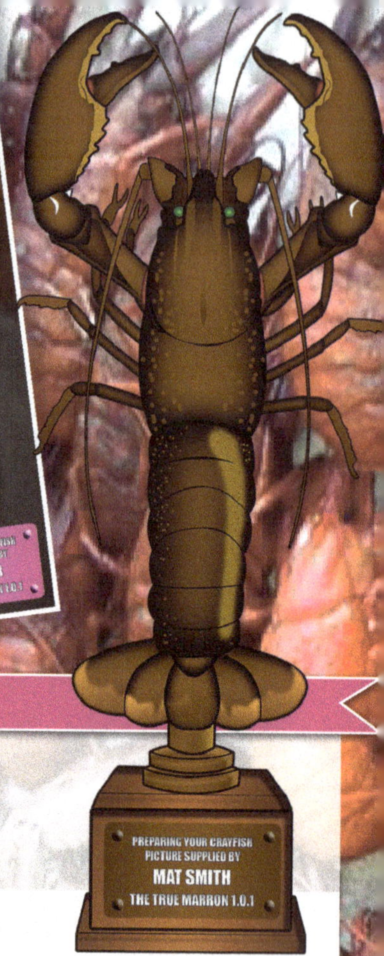

PREPARING YOUR MARRON

DEFROSTING

If using frozen marron, thaw them out by placing them in cold salted water. Drain & discard the water,.

YOU CAN LEAVE YOUR FLAP ON!

- Gently twist the head and pull it from the marron's body.
- Using your fingers, roll off the shell from the underside with the legs still attached to the shell.
- Gently squeeze the tail and carefully remove it. If you wish, the tail flap can remain attached to the body for better presentation.

GETTING RID OF THE GOOEY BIT

Using your fingers, strip out the black intestinal tract (poop shoot) completely. For raw marron, you may need to use a small knife to make a shallow cut along the back before removing the this. It is not a necessity that this is removed.
Giving the crayfish tiny chunks or shredded, easy to eat potato, will have the tract opaque and out of the eyes of the picky. If you need help? Just think of it as a sausage skin with potato inside.

> WE ARE GROWN UPS! IT'S CALLED A 'POOP' SHOOT!

THIS TOPIC BRINGS ME TO BOILING POINT!

Ok! now this is a subject that gets **ALL** peoples knickers in a knot, so I'll try not to offend **ANYONE**.
Yes! We know they are living creatures,
Yes! We know they feel pain,
Yes! We think it un-ethical for **ANY** creature to be put in a cold bath and slowly letting the water boil. Unlike frogs, who will adapt (as the saying goes), marron will not! The meat will become mushy, off-colour and generally is ruined from stress. Not saying frogs don't taste horrible after the same ordeal, but I have never eaten frogs that way either!
But! There is one thing we as individuals seem to forget!
Not everyone has access to a freezer for half an hour and there are times where purging just isn't an option.. Now my water's boiling..

PREPARING YOUR MARRON

PREPARING YOUR CRAYFISH
PICTURE SUPPLIED BY:
MICK GAFNEY
THE TRUE MARRON PL 1

SO! LET'S MAKE THIS EASY!

UNDER 600 GRAMS	10 MINS
600 - 800 GRAMS	12 MINS
800 - 100 GRAMS	14 MINS
1 - 1.5 KILO	16 MINS
1.5 - 2 KILO	18 MINS
3 KILO + OVER	25 MINS

After purging your marron FOR 24 HOURS
(health reasons) from the river or dam. bring a large pot of water to boil (75°C). If you have not had 'the luxury of being able to freeze the bugs first, place them in slowly, head first. Make sure you stop with the marrons head submerged until the tail curls up and the animal is instantly dead. If the water is too cold, your crayfish will flick it large muscle in the tail and potentially free itself from your grip with the force that it creates.
Do not cook more than 6 to 12 crayfish at a time depending on the size of your pot (to many will drop the water temperature).
Cook the crayfish for about 5 minutes (between 2 & 10 minutes, depending on their size). Begin timing as soon as the water returns to a rolling boil (75°C) after the dropping of the last crayfish in the pot. Your marron are ready when they turn **DARK RED** in colour.

SEE MARK REW'S PERFECTLY COOKED BUGS ON PAGE 61.

EXTRACTING THE FLESH

It is easier to extract flesh after cooking whole Mud-Bugs & Lobsters.
1. Remove head.
2. Cut around the inside edges of the tail with food scissors.
3. Gently lever off the undershell from the head end to the tail end.
4. Remove the meat.

BUTTERFLYING

This is usually done when the marron is still raw. It is used to increase both the visual appeal and the apparent size of the prawns. Cut the shelled prawn lengthwise, almost right through the flesh and along its entire length, traditionally along the stomach. Alternatively, you can cut along the back of the prawn to give a circular shape and larger appearance. It also helps with soking up your marinade. Deveining can be done at the same time as the butterflying.
The tail is traditionally left on for butterfly marron tail.

SPLITTING IN HALF (COOKED OR UNCOOKED)

This is best done by using a heavy-bladed knife and following these steps carefully, be sure to watch your fingers:
- Place the dead animal on its stomach. If it is cooked, the tail can be left curled up. Insert the point of a strong knife through the centre of the body.
- Cut all the way through the body towards the tail with a levering action (mind those fingers).
- Turn the cray around. Reinsert the knife in the centre of the body & cut the head neatly in half between the eyes.
- Gently pull apart and wash under cold running water to remove guts and intestinal tract. The roe and "mustard" can be used in a sauce or served with the dish and can compliment most soups to add a mysterious flavour.

SHOTGUN THE TAILS!

If you only like the tails, simply break the tail away from the body. The tail meat can be removed by slicing the underbelly membrane and folding the shell apart to reveal the flesh. This can be done if they are cooked or uncooked. The claws and head can be used for decoration or frozen to be used again for a Marron Soup.

TIMELESS HILL
MANJIMUP WESTERN AUSTRALIA

IT'S BLACK TRUFFLE HARVEST SEASON AT TIMELESS HILL

Truffles will be in season in June to late August.
Our product is available for tasting and purchase at the

MANJIMUP FARMERS MARKET WESTERN AUSTRALIA

On the 1st and 3rd Saturday mornings of those months.

VISITOR HUNTS ARE AVAILABLE BY APPOINTMENT.

TRUFFLES ARE AVAILABLE FOR PURCHASE BY APPOINTMENT.

Please contact Anne Mitchell, through her website;
WWW.TIMELESSHILL.COM.AU
Special orders and requests can be emailed:
INFO@TIMELESSHILL.COM.AU

101 WAYS TO COOK MARRON

> PRODUCE STRAIGHT FROM THE LAND TO COMPLIMENT OUR GOURMET MUD-BUGS! SEE YOU ALL SOON!

KEEPING THINGS GREEN AWARD — 1.0.2 MARRON

MAZZ & ELI'S FAVOURITE INGREDIENTS

SUBMITTED COMPETITION RECIPES CONTENTS

NICE AND EASY!	MIK STANLEY	70
CHILLI PICKLED MARRON	CHEF MACON	71
NICE AND EASY!	PAUL HARFOUCHE	71
2 PICKLED MARRON	ADAM PURDY	73
THE MANS MARRON	BRONWYN GANDY	73
MARRON BOILED WITH FENNEL FRONDS	CHEF MACON	76
RANCHERS MARRON	MAZZ C. CAINII	78
'MUSH'ROOM LEFT FOR MARRON	HEINRICH	80
PAN-FRIED MARRON	CHEF MACON	83
MACON TRAFFIC STOPPER STICKS	CHEF MACON	84
HONEY & LIME GRILLED MARRON	BERNIE PEARL	87
CORIANDER & LIME BUTTERFLIED MARRON	BERNIE PEARL	87
MARRON WITH GREEN PEPPERCORN & MARTINI SAUCE	LISA FEATHERBY	89
LEMON BBQ MARRON	MICK DE WIT	91
GARLIC BAKED MARRON	CHEF MACON	91
MICKS BBQ BACON MARRON	MICK DE WIT	92
CRAYFISH CAN'T WRAP	CLOVE R. LIC	95
SOUTH-WEST MARRON WRAP	SHANTEL BERGROTH	97
MARRON MUSTARD WRAP	SHANTEL BERGROTH	97
HOME MADE MAYO	MATTHEW WILLIAMS	98
CRAYZ MAYONNAZ	PUCKA CITRON	98
THE MARRON SALSA	SHANTEL BERGROTH	101
MARRON DRESSING	SHANTEL BERGROTH	101

SALT & PEPPER YABBY WITH HOLY BASIL	CLOVE R. LIC	103
MACON FRI-RI	CLOVE R. LIC	103
SAUTÉED MARRON & KESTRAL SPUDS	CLOVE R. LIC	103
SCOUNGERS SALAD	DANY D. LION	104
CRAYFISH SALAD	CLOVE R. LIC	110
CRAY-Z MUSHROOM OMELETTE	MAZZ C. CAINII	111
MAZ AND PIG GRATIN	CLOVE R. LIC	111
BAKED SPUDS STUFFED WITH MAZZ & SNAGS	MAZZ C. CAINII	113
SPUD SACKS STUFFED WITH MACON & CHEESE	CLOVE R. LIC	113
MARRON POTATO SALAD	SHANTEL BERGROTH	114
THE BRAVE, THE BOLD & THE BATTERED	SHANTEL BERGROTH	114
MARRON OPEN SANDWICH WITH LIME MAYO	MAZZ C. CAINII	117
SWEET & SOUR DIPPING SAUCE	ADAM PURDY	119
COCONUT MARRON TAILS	ADAM PURDY	119
MARRON, NATIVE CITRUS & GARDEN SALAD	LIMETTA CITRON	121
CLOVE'S SWEET SALAD	CLOVE R. LIC	121
MAZZ, DR. WALTER MELON & FETTA SALAD	'COBBA'	123
MACON & GREEN PEPPER QUICHE	CHEF MACON	123
HOT TONGUE BUTTON, GREEN BEAN & YABBY SALAD	BERNIE PEARL	125
YABBY A LA BISQUE	ADAM PURDY	126
YABBY & SAMPHIRE STIR FRIED NOODLES	PUCKA CITRON	129
NICE & EASY!	MICK STANLEY	130

COMPETITION RECIPE CONTENTS CONT'D

CHEESY MAZZ & MUSTARD SANGA	MAZZ C. CAINII	131
MARRON CABAPPLE SALAD READY TO GO!	MAZZ C. CAINII	131
SWEET CHILLI 4 MACON & BROCCOLI SALAD	PEPPY RINGBURNER	131
DEEF FRIED MARRON TAIL ROLLS	MATTHEW WILLIAMS	133
NUTTY MACON & SHROOMS	BLAZE PEARL	135
MAZZ & THE RED HOT CHILLI PEPPER SALAD	PEPPY RINGBURNER	135
CAMPFIRE GOOGIE MUSSELS & MARRON TAIL	HEINRICH	136
YABBY & PINEAPPLE STIR-FRY	BLAZE PEARL	137
BUTTONED UP MARRON IN A BLANKET	HEINRICH	138
MAZZ ON A STICK	SHANTEL BERGROTH	138
PIRI-PIRI MARRON ON A STICK	BLAZE PEARL	139
MAZZ'Z BALLS	CLOVE R. LIC	139
NICE AND EASY!	MARK CUZENS	140
MARRON, COCONUT AND LIME LEAF STICKS	LIMETTA CITRON	141
A TIMELESS TRUFFLE, MARRON & KIFLER SALAD	ADAM PURDY	141
TOSSED YABBY SALAD	SYDNEY SEAFOOD SCHOOL	142
MARRON. TRUFFLE & ASPARAGUS SALAD	ADAM PURDY	145
BOOKALAAM MARRON WITH TRUFFLE & MANGO SALAD	ADAM PURDY	149
MARRON 'TORTURE'LLINI	CLOVE R. LIC	153
PADDOCK & POND ON A STICK WITH CHIPS	ADAM PURDY	155
CHIVE & CHEESE SAUCE	PAULA DAVIS	157
GARLIC & LEMON MARRON	PAULA DAVIS	157

NICE AND EASY!	ROBIN CUNNINGHAM	166
CHAR-GRILLED CLOVE WITH CAP-C-YUM & MAZZ	BERNIE PEARL	167
CHILLI MARRON SPAGHETTI	SHANTEL BERGROTH	168
NICE AND EASY!	KANDIE HILL	170
MARRON PARMY	SHANTEL BERGROTH	171
MARRON & DUTCH CHEESE PASTA	SHANTEL BERGROTH	174
MAZZ, PANCETTA & TOM-INION PIZZA	ADAM PURDY	176
SWEET CHILLI YABBY PIZZA	MATTHEW WILLIAMS	177
MUSTARD MARRON PIZZA	SHANTEL BERGROTH	178
SWEET BERRY MARRON PIZZA	SHANTEL BERGROTH	178
DAALINY* PEPPERONI & MARRON PIZZA	BLAZE PEARL	182
GLAMPERS SPICY FLATBREAD	PUCKA CITRON	182
MARRON SOUP WITH RISONI	KANGA' IS. MARRON FARM	184
MARRON HEAD SOUP	RHIANNON COOMBS	185
'COBBA' WITH WEDGES	'COBBA'	188
CAMPFIRE PAN-FRIED 'COBBA' & MAZZ	'COBBA'	189
DRY MARRON COOKUP	LIMETTA CITRON	189
GARLIC GIVES YOU MARRON MUSSELS	ALUNIO CARTERI	191
DRUNKEN MAZZ & GINGER MUSSELS	ALUNIO CARTERI	191
ALUNIOS CREEK FOOD BASKET	ALUNIO CARTERI	192
MARRON & TOMATO RISOTTO	CHEF MACON	194
MARRON SOUP	SHANTEL BERGROTH	194
CRISPY MARRON	KANGA' ISL. MARRON FARM	195
THE UNDROPPABLE FALAFEL	ADAM PURDY	197

NOTES:

> WHY DO CRABS SWIM IN SALT WATER? BECAUSE PEPPER WATER MAKES THEM SNEEZE!

101 WAYS TO COOK MARRON

VINEGAR, LEMON, CHILLI, LITTLE SALT & SOME BLACK PEPPER. BEAUTIFUL! - MIK STANLEY

CHILLI PICKLED MARRON

INGREDIENTS
200g marron meat.
2 teaspoons black peppercorns.
1 red chilli (finely chopped).
1-2 litres white malt vinegar.
1 tablespoon white sugar.

METHOD
In a large pot bring water to the boil. Add marron and bring water back to the boil with marron in.
Allow marron to cook for 1-2 minutes after they float to the top then remove.
Plunge in cold water to stop the cooking process on removal.
De-shell and clean marron before packing in to glass jar.
Meanwhile add all other ingredients (the varieties are endless, check the next page) to a pot and heat to dissolve sugar.
Just before boiling add vinegar mix to the jar until full and covering all the marron.
Secure lid on tight and let stand (the warm vinegar cooling will vacuum seal the lid on the jar). Let stand before consuming.
Marron can store for months pickled and goes perfect in a sandwich or just by itself.

101 WAYS TO COOK MARRON
PICTURE SUPPLIED BY
TANDANUS 'COBBA' BOSKOCKI
THE TRUE MARRON 1.0.1

101 WAYS TO COOK MARRON
RECIPE SUPPLIED BY
CHEF MACON
THE TRUE MARRON 1.0.1

101 WAYS TO COOK MARRON
PICTURE SUPPLIED BY
PAUL HARFOUCHE
THE TRUE MARRON 1.0.1

OI!

I'VE USED GARLIC BUTTER & DILL
- PAUL HARFOUCHE

PICKLED DOT-TO-DOT

Pickling marron is pretty simple and the different flavour combinations to be had are endless. Marron is one of those meats that absorb the flavours it is in, adding to that soft texture we all love so much.

Pickling the marron meat is one of the most common methods of eating this delicacy so it really comes down to your preferred taste buds with flavour. To make it easier we have supplied a dot-to-dot of ingredients that make for the perfect any-time snack. Plus some room to add your own concoctions at the bottom. Time to get **PICKLED**.

WHY DO WE REFER TO PROBLEMS AS PICKLES? I LIKE PICKLES!

1ST INGREDIENT:	2ND INGREDIENT:	PICKLING LIQUIDS:
Basil	o Tumeric o	White Wine
Bay Leaf	o Lemon Zest o	Red Wine
Black Pepper	o Lime Zest o	White Vinegar
Chilli Flakes	o Orange Zest o	Brown Wine
Cilantro	o Lemon Pepper o	Spiced Malt Vinegar
Coriander	o Steak Spice o	White Wine Vinegar
All Spice	o Chicken Stock o	Balsamic Vinegar
Black Salt	o Black Salt o	French Dressing
Cayenne Pepper	o Cayenne Pepper o	Italian Dressing
Chives	o Sugar o	Coconut Oil
Cumin	o Paprika o	Truffle Oil
Dill	o Saffron o	Chicken Stock
Fennel	o Thyme o	Beef Stock
Garlic Ginger	o Seven Spice o	Apple Cider
Onion	o Lemon Grass o	
Onion Flakes	o Cajun o	
Oregano	o Coconut o	White Wine
Salt	o Basil o	Red Wine
Sugar	o Dill o	White Vinegar
Paprika	o Fennel o	Brown Wine
Saffron	o Garlic Ginger o	Spiced Malt Vinegar
Thyme	o Bay Leaf o	White Wine Vinegar
Seven Spice	o Chives o	Balsamic Vinegar
Tumeric	o Cumin o	French Dressing
Lemon Zest	o Onion o	Italian Dressing
Lime Zest	o Oregano o	Coconut Oil
Orange Zest	o Salt o	Truffle Oil
Lemon Pepper	o Black Pepper o	Chicken Stock
Steak Spice	o Chilli Flakes o	Beef Stock
Chicken Stock	o Onion Flakes o	Apple Cider
Lemon Grass	o Cilantro o	
Cajun	o Coriander o	
Coconut	o All Spice o	

2 PICKLED MARRON

INGREDIENTS
3/4 cup spiced malt vinegar.
30ml white wine.
1/2 tsp dry basil (or 1 tsp fresh chopped).
1/2 tsp parsley.
1 red chilli.
4 cloves of garlic.

METHOD
Mix together well & pour over RAW flesh and shake well. Should be ready in 2 days.

101 WAYS TO COOK MARRON RECIPE SUPPLIED BY ADAM PURDY THE TRUE MARRON 1.0.1

THE MANS MARRON

INGREDIENTS
400g marron meat.
2 litres vinegar.
2 litres of water.
1/4 cup of salt.
1/4 cup pickling spice.
6 to 8 chopped dried red chilles.
1 onion sliced.
6 to 8 cloves of garlic.
Juice of 2 lemons.

METHOD
Boil marron 3 to 4 minutes in water until ready, then allow to cool. Combine 2 litres of water, vinegar, salt, pickling spice, onion, garlic, chilli and lemon juice in a large stock pot and boil for 30 minutes. Allow to cool before placing marron in the brine and allow to pickle for at least 24 hours.

101 WAYS TO COOK MARRON RECIPE SUPPLIED BY BRONWYN GANDY THE TRUE MARRON 1.0.1

SWITCH BETWEEN SALT & LEMON TO COMPLIMENT YOUR DESIRED FLAVOURS.
CRAY-Z IS AS CRAY-Z DOES
THE TRUE MARRON
1.0.1
Adam J Purdy

MARRON BOILED WITH FENNEL FRONDS

TYPICAL! FORGOT ME OUT OF THIS ONE TOO!

INGREDIENTS
Large handful cooking salt.
8 yabbies or 3-5 marron per person.
Large handful fennel fronds.
Bread spread with mayonnaise.

METHOD
Bring a very large saucepan of water to the boil, then add salt and stir well.
Add marron or yabbies and fennel fronds and cook for 2 minutes (depending on size) or until meat is just cooked (test by twisting off the head.) When cooked, remove from water and cool slightly. Twist off heads, pull out digestive tracts, peel and slice each tail. Place tails on bread with mayo. Eat while still warm.

RECIPE SUPPLIED BY: CHEF MACON
PICTURE SUPPLIED BY: MICK DE WIT

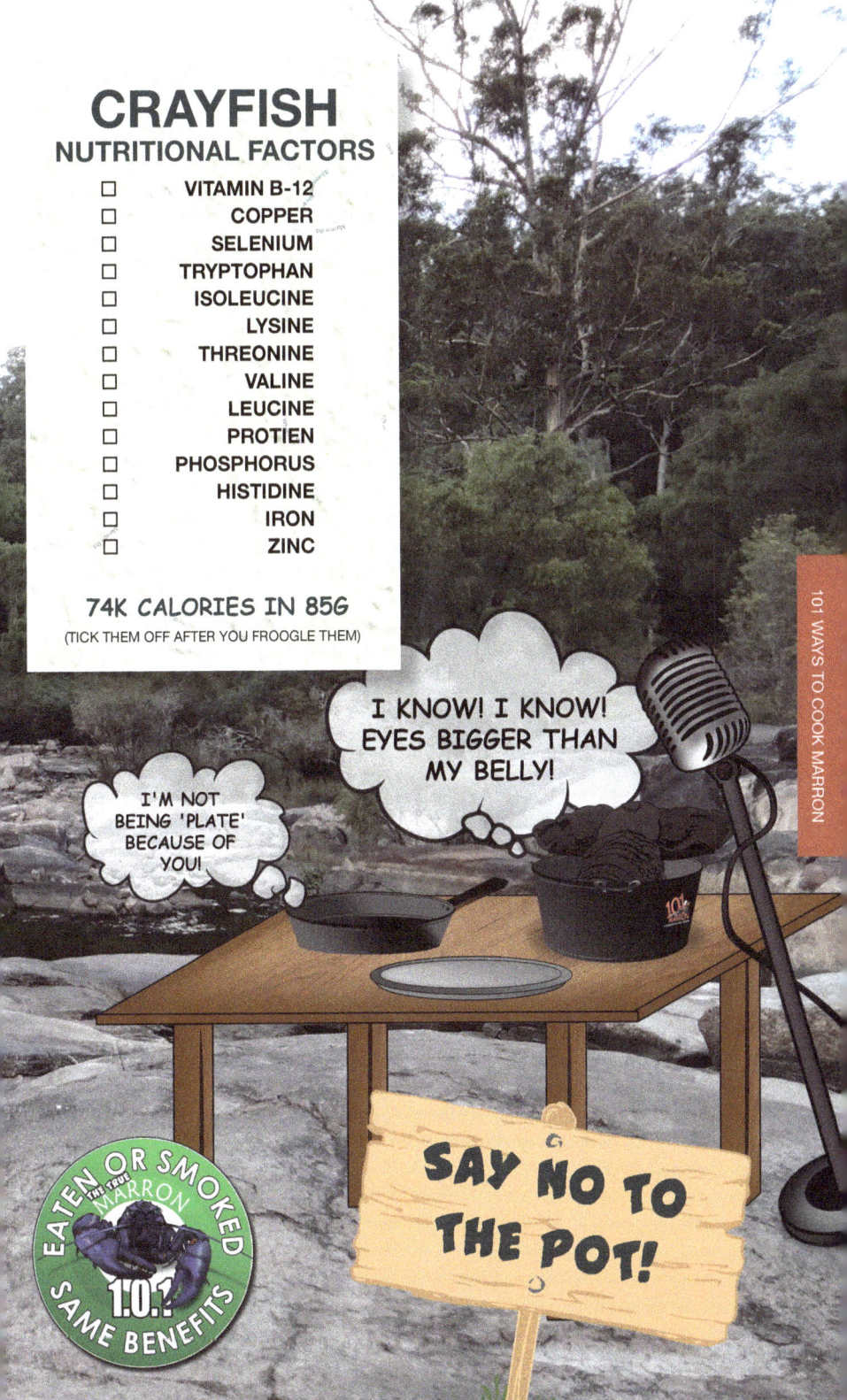

RANCHERS MARRON

INGREDIENTS
2 bunches broccolini.
6 cloves of garlic.
1/2 cup baby endive.
8 cherry tomatoes.
2 live marron.
90g parmesan, grated.
40g cheese, grated.
100g firm goat's curd, diced.
250ml pure cream.
100ml milk.
1/2 cup croutons.
30g plain flour.
30g butter.
Olive oil for drizzling.

METHOD
Bring milk & cream to the boil.
Blanch stems then finely slice the broccolini.
In another saucepan, melt butter over medium heat and add flour.
Cook, stirring, until golden.
Slowly add hot milk and cream, whisking regularly, until thick.
Add garlic, parmesan, cheese and broccolini heads & stems.
Stand to cool.
Place marron in iced water for 20 minutes to put to sleep.
Meanwhile bring 2 litres salted water to the boil.
Add marron, bring back to the boil and simmer for 6 minutes.
Drain. Cool slightly then cut in half lengthways.
For salad, combine goat's curd, tomatoes, croutons, endive, and 6 stems of broccolini.
Drizzle with olive oil. Place marron in a baking dish and spoon over broccolini and cheese sauce mix. Sprinkle with remaining parmesan. Bake at 200°C for 10 minutes until golden.

SERVE WITH SALAD & ROASTED GARLIC CLOVE.

THIS'TLE' FIX HER WAGON!

'MUSH'ROOM LEFT FOR MARRON

INGREDIENTS
1 medium size marron.
Assorted mushrooms.
Vine leaves.
Verjuice.
Shallots.
Lemon thyme leaves.
Walnut oil.
Butter.

METHOD
Place marron in freezer for 20 minutes to stun.
Next destroy the main nerve centre by inserting a knife into the central ridge of the head between the eyes and levering the knife downwards.
Bring large pot of water to boil and plunge marron totally immersed for 2 minutes. Remove from pot and allow to cool.
Mix chopped shiitake mushrooms with walnut oil and a little bit of verjuice.
Put a '**DOB**' of butter on each vine leaf and put mushrooms and vine leaves on tray together and cook in a hot oven for 3 to 5 minutes.
Remove tray, take cook vine leaves off and return Shiitakes to the hot oven for another 5 to 7 minutes.
Mince shallots, lemon and thyme leaves with walnut oil to make a paste.
Cut marron in half down the middle and rub the paste into the flesh.
Leave to marinate while the mushrooms cook. Remove mushrooms from oven, put some butter on the marron tails and add the two Marron halves to the pan shell up (butter down).
Put back into the oven for 2 to 3 minutes. Serve marron with shiitake and juice from the tray and garnish with vine leaves.

WHY DON'T CRAYFISH SHARE? BECAUSE THEY ARE 'SHELL'FISH!

101 WAYS TO COOK MARRON

PAN-FRIED MARRON

BACON & MARRON HMMMM?? THIS IS MAKING ME HUNGRY! MACON! THIS IS 'MACON' ME HUNGRY!

INGREDIENTS
2 marron (large) cut in half.
White balsamic vinegar.
Butter.
Shallots.
Garlic.
Bay leaf.
1 Lime.

METHOD
Cut Marron in half.
Grate lemon zest over marron halves.
Place a good dob of butter on each tail and squeeze lime juice over.
Place two halves of the marron in a hot pan shell up and place lid on. Steam the marron with the butter.
Marron should be a deep red when cooked.
Dash with white balsamic vinegar to keep it moist.
Place the two halves of the marron on a plate.
Put a bit of butter on the tail and cover with alfoil to keep moist while you make the syrup.
Crush and combine shallots, garlic, bay leaf and the other half marron halves in the pan to combine flavours. Add a squeeze of lime and a nob of butter. Continue with the butter and lime until condensed into a nice syrup texture.
Drizzle the dressing over the marron halves to serve.

101 WAYS TO COOK MARRON
RECIPE SUPPLIED BY
CHEF MACON
THE TRUE MARRON 1.0.1

I REMEMBER MY GREAT GRAND-CRABBY TELLING ME STORIES OF HIS FRIENDS GETTING BAKED BY THE FIRE.. (DEEP SIGH) COULD NEVER UNDERSTAND WHY HE ALWAYS CRIED WHEN HE TOLD IT??

MACON TRAFFIC STOPPER STICKS

INGREDIENTS
1 red capsicum.
1 yellow capsicum.
1 green capsicum.
7 tbsp olive oil.
1 tsp dried oregano.
300g smoked ham.
300g precooked marron tail.
8 rashers of diced bacon.
300g diced mixed mushrooms.
1 tsp oregano.
1 tsp cumin powder.
2 tbsp of warmed honey.

METHOD
Soak your wooden skewers in cold water for 20 minutes.
Cut the capsicums, mushroo smoked ham & marron tails into inch sized chunks.
Thread the skewers: red, ham, yellow, mushroom, green, marron.
Mix the cumin, oregano, garlic, warmed honey with 4 tablespoons of olive oil and drizzle it over the skewers.
Allow to marinate for 20 minutes.
Grill the kebabs for 4-5 minutes or until honey is starting to caramelise on the marron.
Meanwhile, fry shredded bacon and mushrooms in the 3 tablespoons of olive oil and oregano for around 8 minutes or until slightly crispy.
Be sure all the oil is evaporated before tipping it onto a warm large serving plate.
Position kebabs on top of bacon & mushroom mix. Garnish with a little more of the warm honey & garlic sauce.
Dress with torn parsley or coriander.

HONEY & LIME GRILLED MARRON

INGREDIENTS
4 large marron tail.
2 black pearl chillies.
2 sliced limes.
2 tbsp honey.
2 tbsp soy sauce.

METHOD
Finely slice the black pearl chillis, put them in a microwave safe container with the honey.
Heat the chilli & honey in the microwave to make it runny.
Mix the syrup with the soy sauce in a freezer bag, stir in the limes.
Add marron tails to the freezer bag and lightly massage marinade.
Preheat the grill.
Let marinade sit for 25 minutes.
Arrange the marron tails and lime slices on a grill tray, grill for 3 minutes on each side or until the honey glaze is golden and sticky and the marron tails are cooked through.
Place marron and lime wedges on a warm plate then drizzle with remaining marinate.
Garnish with spring onion.

WHAT A 'LIME' RECIPE! IF I WAS THE GARLIC, I'D BE CRUSHED TOO!

CORIANDER & LIME BUTTERFLIED MARRON

INGREDIENTS
4 x 500g red marron.
2 tbsp Bookalaam Olive Oil.
Coriander sprigs.
Lime wedges.
150g butter, cubed, (room temperature).
1/3 cup coriander leaves, chopped.
1/4 tsp ground paprika.
Juice & finely grated zest of 1 lime.
1 garlic clove, crushed.

METHOD
Butterfly the marron and pat the insides off with paper towel. To make the lime & coriander butter, place all the ingredients in a food processor and process until smooth. Lay a piece of baking paper on a chopping board and spoon butter mixture onto the centre. Use the paper to shape into a log, then roll up to enclose and twist the ends to seal. Chill until required, then unroll and gently cut into 1cm-thick slices. Preheat a barbecue grill or char-grill pan on high.
Brush cut sides of Marron with oil. Season. Cook, cut-side down, for 1-2 mins or until lightly browned.
Turn and top each Marron half with slices of butter mixture. Cook, shell-side down, for 1-2 mins or until heated through.
Serve with coriander, lime wedges and extra butter, if desired.

101 WAYS TO COOK MARRON
RECIPE SUPPLIED BY
BERNIE PEARL
THE TRUE MARRON I.D.1

MARRON WITH GREEN PEPPERCORN & MARTINI SAUCE

INGREDIENTS
8 live black marron.
100 grams of butter, melted.

TO GARNISH
Salad burnet or chervil sprigs.

TO SERVE
Sourdough rye bread & green salad.
1 tbsp green peppercorn and martini sauce.
Fresh green peppercorns crushed.
4 red shallots, finely chopped.
125ml (½ cup) dry vermouth.
180 grams of butter, diced & softened.
1 tbsp lemon juice.
1 tbsp vodka.
1 tbsp coarsely chopped chervil.

METHOD

Meanwhile for green peppercorn and martini sauce, combine peppercorns, shallot and vermouth in a small saucepan, bring to the boil over high heat, then simmer over medium heat for 5 minutes or until reduced to 2 tbsp. Reduce heat to low and whisking continuously,

gradually add butter, one piece at a time, until it's all combined and sauce has emulsified. (Don't let sauce get too hot or it will split.) Add lemon juice and vodka, whisk to combine, stir through chervil and season to taste with sea salt and freshly ground black pepper. Set aside and keep warm.

Preheat grill to high, season marron to taste, brush with melted butter and grill for 5 minutes or until just cooked through.

To serve, arrange marron on a platter, spoon sauce over, garnish with salad burnet and serve immediately with bread and green salad to the side.

Salad burnet is a herb with a taste similar to cucumber available from select greengrocers.

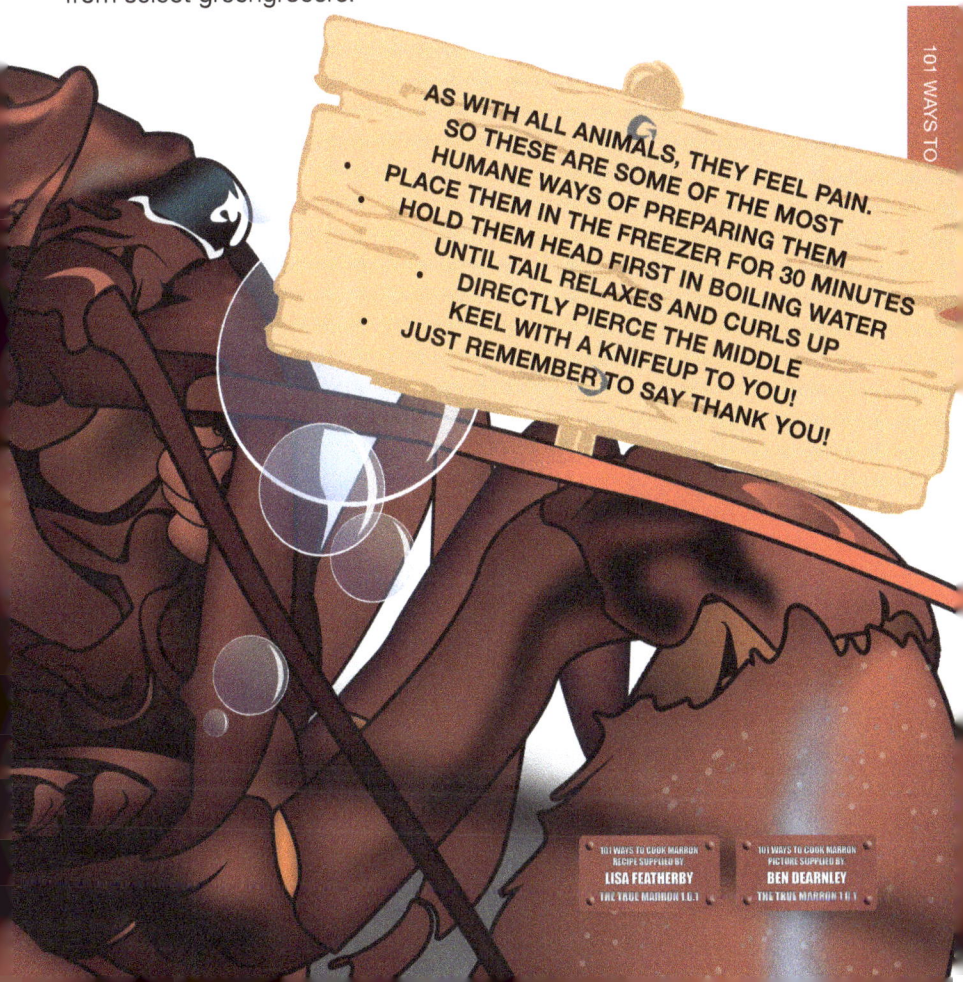

AS WITH ALL ANIMALS, THEY FEEL PAIN. SO THESE ARE SOME OF THE MOST HUMANE WAYS OF PREPARING THEM
- PLACE THEM IN THE FREEZER FOR 30 MINUTES
- HOLD THEM HEAD FIRST IN BOILING WATER UNTIL TAIL RELAXES AND CURLS UP
- DIRECTLY PIERCE THE MIDDLE KEEL WITH A KNIFE UP TO YOU!
JUST REMEMBER TO SAY THANK YOU!

101 WAYS TO COOK MARRON RECIPE SUPPLIED BY
LISA FEATHERBY
THE TRUE MARRON T.D.T

101 WAYS TO COOK MARRON PICTURE SUPPLIED BY
BEN DEARNLEY
THE TRUE MARRON T.D.T

AHH! ANOTHER BEAUTY FROM MICK DE WIT! WHO'S HUNGRY?
CRAY-Z IS AS CRAY-Z DOES
THE TRUE MARRON
Adam T Purdy

A 'PURDY' GOOD TIP: PREPARING THE TAILS IS A GREAT WAY TO GET ALL THE FAMILY INVOLVED

LEMON BBQ MARRON

INGREDIENTS
1kg of marron.
1 Lemon.
Lemon thyme.
Garlic butter.
Salt 'n' pepper.
Zest of 1 lemon.
Olive oil.

METHOD
Prep marron by cutting in half, take out poop shoot, put marron on medium heat hot plate shell side up with lemon zest, garlic butter & lemon thyme for 1 minute to seal in the lovely flavours. Turn over marron then drizzle over with olive oil. Salt and pepper to taste, cover with aluminium foil for about 8 to 10 minutes, remove aluminium foil then drizzle with the juice of the lemon over all the marron & serve.

101 WAYS TO COOK MARRON RECIPE SUPPLIED BY **MICK DE WIT** *THE TRUE MARRON 1.0.1*

GARLIC BAKED MARRON

INGREDIENTS
16 x 75g red marron.
100g butter.
2 cloves garlic, finely chopped.
1 tablespoon chopped flat-leaf parsley leaves.
1 lemon, zested and juiced.
Salt flakes.
Freshly ground black pepper.

METHOD
Preheat the oven to 200°C. Melt the butter in a small saucepan. Add garlic, parsley, lemon zest and juice, salt and pepper and stir to combine. Halve marron lengthways, from the head down through the tail. Remove head contents, devein and arrange, flesh-side up, on a baking tray. Brush liberally with the butter mixture. Bake for 3-5 minutes, until the flesh is opaque and shells have turned orange. Arrange marron on plates and drizzle with the cooking juices and any remaining butter mixture.

101 WAYS TO COOK MARRON RECIPE SUPPLIED BY **CHEF MACON** *THE TRUE MARRON 1.0.1*

CRUSTY BREAD & GREEN SALAD TO SERVE.

MICKS BBQ BACON MARRON

INGREDIENTS
Bacon.
Lemon.
Marron.
Lemon thyme.
Butter.
Herbal sprinkle.
Salt 'n' pepper.

MICK'S TIP: BEST SERVED WITH A COLD TOOHEY'S NEW WHILE HANGING WITH MATES!

METHOD
Put marron to sleep in freezer.
Break tails off then cut under tail in half longways and remove poop shoot.
Cut up bacon strips for every piece of marron meat.
Pre heat hot plate, put butter on with bacon for 2 mins each side.
Place marron shell side down, season marron meat with lemon thyme, herbal sprinkle & salt n pepper.
Cook until marron meat starts to turn white.
Place marron meat side onto bacon pieces to soak up the flavours for 5 minutes.
Just before removing marron drizzle half a lemon over the lot.

CUMMON! BE A FUN-GUY & TOSS A FEW OF US IN!

PICTURE SUPPLIED BY BRETT COOK

MEAT TROUDY - OUR LOCAL 'CELERY'ITY JUDGE

Hey Everyone! My name is Troudy and you can find me at Old Vasse Trout & Marron Farm. A lot of recreational anglers fish for rainbow trout and also our cousin the brown trout.
We are now found in rivers and other freshwater bodies in the south-west of Western Australia.
Both of our families were bought here and introduced to Australia, through the Pemberton Freshwater Research Centre, who annually restock the south-west waterways with both species of trout.
Anglers aged 16 and over require a freshwater angling licence to fish in freshwater streams and riverways. Come to Old Vasse Trout & marron farm and you can fish for us all year long!
Mazz and I have both been under the spotlight since around 1962. Before we came around Cobba's Family was very popular with the natives and locals of the region. Restaurants, Bars & Clubs all like to serve a good platter of either of us with a good basket of chips!
I would love to invite you all to come see Mazz & I at Old Vasse Trout & Marron Farm with the **'OFF THE ROAD'** Crew from **ON THE HUNT FOR THE TRUE MARRON.**
They will be doing presentations and shows teaching the public everything they need to know, right on the banks of the farms picturesque dam.

A PERFECT LOCATION FOR:
WEDDINGS & FUNCTIONS
BUS TOUR GROUPS

www.oldvassetroutandmarron.com.au

Check Out
WWW.THETRUEMARRON101.AU
FOR OUR FULL RANGE OF MERCHANDISE.
WE DO CUSTOM DESIGNS TOO!

> PFFFT! YEAH? AND WHITE MEN CAN'T JUMP RIGHT?

101 WAYS TO COOK MARRON
RECIPES SUPPLIED BY
CLOVE R. LIC
THE TRUE MARRON 1.0.1

CRAYFISH CAN'T WRAP

INGREDIENTS
200g crayfish tails.
6 soft tortillas.
Grated zest of 1 lime.
1½ tbsp chopped coriander.
2 tbsp mayonnaise.
½ tsp paprika.
1 mango, finely sliced.
120g washed spinach leaves.
2 tsp green jalapeño sauce.

METHOD
Mix mayonnaise with the green jalapeño sauce, and zest of lime with coriander, sliced mango and paprika.
Add the crayfish to the mayonnaise mixture.
Place spinach leaves onto the wrap and place 1/4 of the mixture onto the wrap and roll up.

BLACK PEARL PEPPERS
When you think of Black Pearls its easy for the mind to float towads a large ghost ship of a famous movie franchise or of some unique, rare piece of jewelery: I think the very same for this Pepper variety. It's a jewel. With its deep purple leaves and small beautiful pearls suitable for a necklace. – They would have to be one of the worlds most beautiful plants, their midnight purple colour pops in salads and stir-fries. Beware though, it comes with a surprising burst of heat of 10,000 to 30,000 Scoville Heat Units (**SHU**s).

SOUTH-WEST MARRON WRAP

INGREDIENTS
Herb and garlic feta.
Spicy red sauce.
Mayonnaise.
Bacon.
Marron.

FAVOURITE SALAD FILLINGS:
Carrot, tomato, lettuce, capsicums, alfalfa sprouts, shaved cucumber.

METHOD
Fry some bacon, add in some marron & lightly fry. Lightly spread herb and garlic feta all over wrap.
Mix a tablespoon of both spicy red sauce and mayonnaise together, then spread all over wrap. Start to layer your favourite salad fillings, add cheese, then bacon and your marron fold or roll your wrap.

MARRON & FUN-GUY WRAP

INGREDIENTS
Wrap of your choice.
Garlic aoli.
½ tsp mustard.
Garlic.
Mushrooms.
Diced marron chunks.
Your favourite salad fillings.

METHOD
Mix garlic aoli and 1/2 tsp of mustard and spread all over the wrap.
Flavour with your favourite salads.
Cook mushrooms in desired amount of garlic.
Toss marron chunks into the garlic mushroom mix to absorb flavour.

ROCK 'N' ROLL & SERVE.

...AND STAY OUT!

HOME MADE MAYO

INGREDIENTS
1 large egg yolk.
1 1/2 teaspoons fresh lemon juice.
1 teaspoon white wine vinegar.
1/4 teaspoon Dijon mustard.
1/2 teaspoon salt (to taste).
3/4 cup canola oil, divided.

METHOD
Combine egg yolk, lemon juice, vinegar, mustard, and salt in a medium bowl. Whisk until blended and bright yellow, usually takes 30 seconds.
Mix 1/4 oil to yolk mix, whisking constantly a few drops at a time for about 4 minutes. Gradually add remaining 1/2 cup oil in slowly, still whisking as you go until mayonnaise is thick.
COVER AND CHILL.

101 WAYS TO COOK MARRON
RECIPE SUPPLIED BY:
MATTHEW WILLIAMS
THE TRUE MARRON T.O.T

CRAYZ MAYONNAZ

INGREDIENTS
2 large eggs yolks.
1 teaspoon of lemon juice.
¼ teaspoon salt.
¼ teaspoon white pepper.
150ml vegetable oil.
150ml light olive oil.
1 teaspoon cold water.

METHOD
Place egg yolks, lemon juice, salt and pepper in a small bowl, whisking to combine.
In a medium jug combine the two oils and water together.
Whisking the yolk mixture vigorously, slowly drizzle in small amounts of the oil mixture, until it has all been incorporated.
Whisk in the crayfish mustard.
PERFECT FOR SANDWICHES & SALADS.

> I DON'T HAVE A TEASPOON, PERHAPS JUST DAB IT ON MY FOREHEAD!

101 WAYS TO COOK MARRON
RECIPE SUPPLIED BY:
PUCKA CITRON
THE TRUE MARRON T.O.T

THE MARRON SALSA

INGREDIENTS
Diced marron.
Tomatoes.
Can of diced tomatoes.
Capsicum.
Onion.
Zuchini.
Chilli.
Garlic.
1/4 cup balsamic vinegar.

METHOD
Dice tomatoes, capsicum, onion, zuchini, pan fry for 3 minutes.
Add chilli, garlic, pepper & balsamic vinegar.
Fry for a further 1 min.
Add can of diced tomatoes, simmer for 6 minutes.
Turn off heat, add diced marron.
give it a good stir.
Put lid on. Serve hot or cold.

MARRON DRESSING

INGREDIENTS
1/2 olive oil.
1/2 cup vinegar.
Chopped parsley.
1 diced onion.
Diced marron.
Slice of lemon or lemon juice.

METHOD
Combine all ingredients in a jar.
Shake well.
Pour over salad or cold boiled spuds.

SIMPLE!

SALT & PEPPER YABBY WITH HOLY BASIL

INGREDIENTS
2 tbsp of minced garlic.
2 tbsp vegetable oil.
1 red chilli.
15-20 peeled yabby with tails intact.
1 tsp of peppercorns.
1/2 tsp sea salt flakes.
1 tsp sugar.
Handful of holy basil leaves.

METHOD
Heat oil in a wok and fry the garlic & chilli for 1 minute.
Add the yabbies and stir-fry over a high heat until yabby flesh is opaque. Stir in pepper, salt and basil.

MACON FRI-RI

INGREDIENTS
400g of marron pieces.
250g of bacon strips.
3 tbsp of olive oil.
1 finely chopped red chilli.
2 cloves of garlic.
50g bean sprouts.
200g sugar snap peas.
1 sliced red capsicum.
2 tbsp soy sauce.
300g mixed rice, cooked & cooled.

METHOD
Heat oil in a wok and fry the garlic and chilli for 1 minute.
Add the marron & bacon **(MACON)** and stir-fry over a high heat until marron flesh is opaque or roughly 3 minutes.
Add rice and stir-fry until piping hot.
Add the soy and bean sprouts and cook for another minute to allow the beans to soak up a little of the soy.

SAUTÉED MARRON & KESTRAL SPUDS

INGREDIENTS
700g of kestral potatoes, chunks.
200g marron tails precooked, chunks.
4 tbsp olive oil.
1 tsp ground cumin.
2 tbsp fresh thyme leaves.

METHOD
Boil kestral potatoes in salted water for 8 minutes, drain well. Leave to steam dry for 2 mins. Heat the oil in a large pan. Sprinkle marron tails and potatoes with cumin, thyme and go to town on the salt & pepper. Fry for 10 minutes.

SCROUNGERS SALAD

101 WAYS TO COOK MARRON RECIPE SUPPLIED BY:
CLOVE R. LIC
THE TRUE MARRON L.O.T

101 WAYS TO COOK MARRON PICTURE SUPPLIED BY:
DANY D. LION
THE TRUE MARRON L.O.T

INGREDIENTS
200g of large marron, peeled with tails intact.
150g of small, peeled yabbies.
1 red onion cut into thin wedges.
300g of cherry tomatoes.
4 tbsp olive oil.
200g of washed fresh samphire.
1 red or purple chilli pepper.
Grapes or Sultan-A's.
Garlic cloves to taste.
Your choice of Fun-Guy.
Handful of almonds (your choice of nuts).
Handful of dandelion leaves.
Watercress and dandelion flowers.

METHOD
Mix the tomatoes and onion in a large baking dish with olive oil. Bake for as long as it takes your fire to caramelise (without burning the onion) and make the tomatoes soft.
Chop the samphire into inch long sections and combine with the almonds, garlic and chosen chilli. Stir in the yabbies and return to the camp oven for 15 minutes or until the yabbies are cooked. Garnish with grapes or Sultan-A's, mushrooms, your choice of nuts, watercress, dandelion leaves and dandelion flower to add a little colour.

OH! DO I HAVE SOME GOSSIP FOR YOU!

DANDELION LEAF BENEFITS
The leaves are used to stimulate the appetite and help digestion. Dandelion flower has antioxidant properties. Dandelion may also help improve the immune system. Herbalists use dandelion root to detoxify the liver and gallbladder, and dandelion leaves to help kidney function.
Great to keep handy on those camping trips.
Just remember: **'WEED'** translates to **'CULL'** in Latin on both sides on the translations to **WESTERN ENGLISH of 25BC-50BC**.

PURDY 'CRAW'FUL JOKES

I NEED MY MORNING 'CLAW'FFEE.

WHY DPN'T MARRON LIKE TENNIS?
BECAUSE THEY ARE AFRAID OF THE NET!

MAZZ & ELI WERE PLAYING HIDE & SEEK.
ELI KEPT YELLING "I SEA YOU! I SEA YOU!

CHECK OUT OUR MERCHANDISE WHEN YOU START THINKING ABOUT SANTA 'CLAWS' THIS YEAR!

WHY DOES MAZZ WANT TO MARRY A PERENNIAL?
HE DOESN'T LIKE THE ADDICTIVE FEMALE 'CRAYS' OF 'SHELL'FIES

WHAT'S MAZZ'S FAVOURITE DRINK?
'CRAB'ACCINO.

SOMETIMES I FEEL LIKE A LOST 'CLAWS' COMING UP WITH THESE PUNS!

THE 'SHELL'FISH CRAY STILL A'PIERS' TO BE CRAY'SEA'.

I HOPE A FEW OF THESE 'CRAB' YOUR ATTENTION?

MAZZ ASKED COBBA WHO HIS COD-FATHER WAS.
APPARENTLY HE IS A 'CRAW'FESSIONAL CHEF.

SOME OF THESE PUNS ARE 'SPRIMP'LY THE BEST DON'T YOU THINK?

DEFINATELY ONE 'SHELL' OF A BOOK!

HEY PUCKA! MAZZ & I JOINED A GYM LAST WEEK!

SWEET! HOW DID YOU GO?

MAZZ DIDN'T LAST LONG, HE PULLED A 'MUSSEL'.

CRAYFISH SALAD

101 WAYS TO COOK MARRON
RECIPE SUPPLIED BY:
CLOVE R. LIC
THE TRUE MARRON 1 O 1

CRAYFISH CONTAIN LOW FATS & CARBOHYDRATES WHICH ARE GREAT FOR WEIGHT LOSS!

INGREDIENTS
750g marron tails or equal weight.
2 ½ tbsp tarragon vinegar.
2 tsp lemon juice.
3 ½ tbsp olive oil.
2 tsp finely chopped tarragon.
80g micro greens.
250g mixed salad leaves.
Sea salt and white pepper
to taste.

METHOD
Put a pot of salted water on to boil.
(Be sure to check our: **MAKE IT EASY** section page 59)
Clean the crayfish tails, removing the vein *cough '**poop shoot**'.
Boil the crayfish tails for 6 to 12 minutes till cooked.
The shell should be a deep red. Remove, drain and allow to cool.
In the meantime, make the salad dressing.
Combine together the tarragon vinegar, lemon juice, olive oil, sea salt & white pepper.
Remove the crayfish flesh from the shell and cut into generous bite size pieces. Fold the crayfish into the dressing,
coating them well.
Arrange the leaves on the platter
Pile the dressed crayfish on top.

SERVE IMMEDIATELY

BOTH ARE GREAT AT HELPING YOU DEAL WHEN YOU'VE HAD A LITTLE TO MUCH OF ME TOO!

GRAPES & SULTANAS
People have cultivated grapes for thousands of years. Grapes offer a wealth of health benefits primarily due to their high nutrient and antioxidant contents. Grapes also make a quick and delicious snack you can enjoy at home or on the go.
Sultanas are commonly eaten on the go, but can be found in most baking recipes as they easily absorb liquid, while still adding a little sweetness to the dish. This added sweet flavour brings a nice fruity surprise (great for the target skeptics to be converted)
You will even find them in chutneys and curries making them, without a doubt, one of the most versatile ingredients in the kitchen.

CRAY-Z MUSHROOM OMELETTE

INGREDIENTS
2 marron.
200g or 2 cups of mixed mushrooms.
Herbs to season.
1 tbsp olive oil.
4 tbsp of butter.
3 large eggs.
1 tbsp chopped chives.

METHOD
Cut mushrooms into pieces. Heat the olive oil and half the butter in a large sauté pan until sizzling nicely. Add the marron & mushrooms, season with salt & pepper. Cook for 10 minutes, stirring occasionally. Crack the eggs into a bowl and gently whisk to break up the yolks. Heat the rest of the butter in a pan, then pour in the eggs and herbs to season. Cook over a medium heat until eggs start to set around the outside edge. Use an eggslice (spatula for the fancy folk!) to move the sides of the omlette into the centre. While tilting the pan to fill the sides with more of the runny egg. Do this until the top of the omlette is set, then fold it over and slide onto a warm plate. Spoon the marron and mushrooms over the omlette and sprinkle with chives.

MAZZ & PIG GRATIN

INGREDIENTS
2 1/2 cups milk.
3 tbsp butter.
1 tbsp plain flour.
3/4 cup grated cheddar cheese.
2 chunky chopped marron.
8 rashers of smoked bacon.
1 large onion, thinly sliced.

THE ONLY THING 'GRATIN' HERE IS MY NERVES WITH ALL THESE PUNS!

METHOD
Preheat oven to 190°C. Heat the butter in a small sausepan then stir in the flour and cook for 1 minute. Preheat the milk. Gradually, while continuously stirring to avoid any lumps forming, add the milk to the sausepan. Continue to stir until it starts to bubble, then stir in the cheese & season with salt & pepper. Arrange the marron, bacon and onion in 4 small gratin dishes then spoon over the sauce. Cook the gratins in the oven for 20mins or until onions are cooked.

BAKED SPUDS STUFFED WITH MAZZ & SNAGS

INGREDIENTS
4 large baking potatoes.
150g shredded marron tail.
6 skinned pork sausages.
1 tbsp wholegrain mustard.
1 crushed garlic clove.

METHOD
Preheat oven to 220°C. Put a few holes in the potatoes with a fork and cook them on high in the microwave for 5 minutes.

Slice off the tops off the potatoes and scoop out the centres with a teaspoon.

Mix the scooped out potato and mix it with the sausage meat and shredded marron tail and stuff it all back into the spud shells. Put the lid back on and bake for 35 minutes or until golden brown and cooked through.

SPUD SACKS STUFFED WITH MACON & CHEESE

INGREDIENTS
4 medium baking potatoes.
2 chopped marron.
2/3 cup chopped bacon.
1 tbsp olive oil.
2 tbsp créme fraiche.
2 tbsp chopped chives.
4 slices french raclette cheese.

METHOD
Preheat oven to 220°C. Put a few holes in the potatoes with a fork and cook them on high in the microwave for 5 minutes.

Meanwhile, fry the chopped marron and bacon **(MACON)** in oil for 5 minutes then stir in the créme fraiche and chives.

Slice the tops off the potatoes and scoop out the centres with a teaspoon. Mix some of the scooped out potato with the marron and bacon mixture, then stuff it back into the potato shells.

Overfill the spud & lay a slice of the French Raclette cheese over each potato. Bake them in the oven for 20 mins or until golden brown.

MARRON POTATO SALAD

INGREDIENTS
Chopped potatoes.
3 Celery stalks.
Mossel chicken stock.
Ham steaks.
3-6 eggs.
Cheese.
Mayonaise.
Carrot.
Pepper.
Diced marron.

METHOD
Boil chopped potatoes and celery in pot of water with chicken stock.
Boil 3-6 eggs, slice ham steaks, grate cheese.
Once potatoes mostly cooked, add broken up eggs, minced ham steaks, diced marron, pepper.
Softly mix with mayonaise.
Mix in grated cheese when ready to serve.

THE BRAVE, THE BOLD & THE BATTERED

INGREDIENTS
110g plain flour.
2 large eggs.
400g of yabby, peeled with tail intact.
Oil for the deep-frier.
Can also be cooked in an air-frier.

WHAT EVER GETS THEM IN THE BELLY FASTER!

METHOD
Heat the oil in a deep fryer to a maximum of 180ºC. Mix the flour with a big pinch of salt & pepper. Make a well in the flour and break in the eggs. Mix up all the flour from the edges with a whisk.
Hold the yabbies by their tails and dip them into the batter then drop them straight into the hot oil. Fry for a few minutes. Line a bowl with kitchen paper to absorb any excess oil. Sprinkle with a little sea salt.
SERVE WITH A SALAD AND CHIPS

A SHORT TRIP - WITH A LONG ENDING

MARRON OPEN SANDWICH WITH LIME MAYO

INGREDIENTS
4 marron (fresh is best, but precooked is fine).
Cooking salt.
2 limes, seeds removed.
Fresh lime juice.
Whole egg mayonnaise.
(**MATT'S HOME MADE**
Recipe is on page 98).
4 slices crusty Italian loaf.
Butter or olive oil.
4 cos lettuce leaves.
Salt for seasoning.
White pepper.

METHOD
Mix 6 tbsp of mayonnaise with 2 tsp lime juice.
Add in 2/3 of the lime peels and taste.
Season further as required (ie: add more juice, salt and pepper).
Coarsely chop half the marron tail meat into large chunks.
Mix with lime mayo until just coated (not swimming) in mayo.
Dress bread by spreading with thin layer of butter, olive oil or lime mayo.

PUTTING IT TOGETHER
Place bread on plate.
Top with cos lettuce leaf.
Add chunks of mayo coated marron.
Carefully balance the remaining (whole) half-tail onto chopped marron.
Season.
Garnish with reserved finger lime pearls (like caviar).

SERVE IMMEDIATELY!

ROW, ROW, ROW YOUR BOAT..

WHILE WE CATCH A FEED!..

MARRONING, MARRONING, MARRONING, MARRONING,

MORE CRAYFISH IS WHAT WE NEED!

SWEET & SOUR DIPPING SAUCE

INGREDIENTS
1 cup sweet & sour sauce.
1 tbsp apple cider vinegar.
1 tbsp chilli garlic sauce.
2 cloves of garlic, minced.

METHOD
Give a light stir to combine.

COCONUT MARRON TAILS

INGREDIENTS
1/4 cup cornstarch.
1 tsp Himalayan salt.
1/2 tsp cayenne pepper.
1 cup canned coconut milk.
1-1/2 cup sweetened, shredded coconut.
1-1/2 cups breadcrumbs.
2 lbs raw marron tails, seasoned with salt and pepper
Canola oil.

METHOD
Whisk together cornstarch, salt, and cayenne in a shallow dish.
Pour coconut milk into another shallow dish.
Combine coconut and panko in the third dish.
Toss raw marron in cornstarch mixture; shake off excess.
Dip the marron in coconut milk, then dredge in coconut mixture pressing to adhere.
Transfer to a plate and chill 1 hour.
Heat about 1 cup canola oil in a large saute pan over medium-high heat. Fry marron in batches until golden brown & cooked through, (1 minute per side is enough). Transfer to a paper-towel lined plate.

SEASON WITH HIMALAYAN SALT.

MARRON, NATIVE CITRUS & GARDEN SALAD

INGREDIENTS
2 marron.
8 bush limes, sliced in half.
2 finger limes.
½ lemon, juiced.
1 cup mixed sweet grass, dandelion leaves & edible flowers & soft herbs.
½ fennel bulb, very thinly sliced.

MAYONNAISE:
1 egg yolk.
2 teaspoons dijon mustard.
½ lemon, juiced.
½ cup (125ml) vegetable oil.

METHOD
Gently remove flesh from tails, and discard intestinal tract. Slice tail meat into 1cm-thick pieces, and place into a bowl. Finely grate the zest of 1 finger lime into the bowl, then add the lime flesh. Add lemon juice and a pinch of salt. Mix well to combine, then set aside to cure.

FOR THE MAYONNAISE
Place egg yolk, mustard and lemon juice in a bowl.
In a slow steady stream, gradually add vegetable oil, whisking vigorously to an emulsified, thick mayonnaise. Add the head flesh of the marron and whisk until combined.
To serve, scatter a platter with half of the fennel, limes, sweet grass, shredded dandelion leaves, flowers and herbs. Smear mayonnaise across platter and arrange marron on top. Dress with remaining fennel & herbs.

CLOVE'S SWEET SALAD

INGREDIENTS
1-2 pre-cooked mazz tails.
2 cups dandelion leaves.
1/2 cup fennel, julienned.
thinly sliced sweet grass.
1/2 julienned apple.
1/4 cup Sultan A's.
Fennel tops.
1/4 cup walnuts.
Balsamic for dressing.
Edible flowers (optional).

METHOD
Combine the all ingredients except the dressing and edible flowers and toss to combine. Drizzle with balsamic and sprinkle with flowers .

ENJOY!

ROAST UP MY ROOTS TO ADD A NUTTY FLAVOUR!

HEY UNCLE? IS IT JUST ME OR IS IT HOT?
MAZZ HAS GOT UNDER MY SKIN! HE HAS NOT LEFT THE TROPHIES SINCE OUR LAST SPOILED PLAN!
UGH! FIND! LOOK HERE!
IS GOOD BOOK, PURDY PICTURES!
UGH, YOU GENIUS! WHY DIDN'T I THINK OF THAT? RALLY THE DJOOL ARMY!
101 WAYS TO COOK MARRON
BIG BLUE AWARD
FOREST FRESH MARRON
THE TRUE MARRON 1.0.1
101 WAYS TO COOK MARRON
LIP BURNER AWARD
SHANTEL BERGROTH
THE TRUE MARRON 1.0.1
PREPARING YOUR CRAYFISH
PICTURE SUPPLIED BY
MAT SMITH
THE TRUE MARRON 1.0.1
JUSTIN OSHEA
THE TRUE MARRON 1.0.1
GAVIN ROBINSON
THE TRUE MARRON 1.0.1
THOSE TROPHIES ARE AS GOOD AS MINE!
UGH HAS AN IDEA!

MAZZ, DR. WALTER MELON & FETTA SALAD

INGREDIENTS
200g precooked yabby tail.
1/4 of a watermelon.
2 cut in half & sliced red onion.
4 tbsp shredded mint leaves.
100g fetta cheese.

METHOD
Use a melon baller to scoop out the watermelon and toss them in with the yabby tail, fetta, mint and onion.

GIVE IT A GOOD MIX & SERVE AS IS..

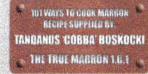

MACON & GREEN PEPPER QUICHE

INGREDIENTS
100g shredded marron tail.
2 rashers thinly sliced bacon.
1 tbsp shredded basil.
2 tbsp olive oil.
6 eggs.

METHOD
Preheat the oven to 180°C
Fry the marron, bacon and peppers in the oil for 10 minutes or until cooked through.
Lightly beat the eggs and stir in the marron, bacon and peppers.
Pour mixture into a non-stick pan and bake for 20 -25 minutes or until quiche is set in the centre.
Sprinkle with the shredded basil and serve warm.

HOT TONGUE BUTTON, GREEN BEAN & YABBY SALAD

INGREDIENTS
15 yabbies, peeled tails intact.
2-3 sliced black pearl peppers.
Handful of sultanas.
200g trimmed green beans.
1 crushed Clove of garlic.
1 tsp of cayenne Peppy.
3 tsp olive oil.
1 tbsp lemon juice.
Parmesan cheese to taste.
Coriander and sliced button mushrooms to garnish it.

METHOD
Preheat the grill.
blanch beans in salted boilng water for 4 minutes, plunge into cold water & drain well.
Mix garlic, sliced black pearl, button mushrooms and cayenne pepper with 2 tbsp of the oil in a feezer bag and massage the paste into the mix. Let sit for 10 minutes to absorb flavours.
Spread yabbies & roomies on a grill tray and grill each side for 2 minutes on each side or tails are cooked through.
Mix lemon juice with the rest of the oil and season well with salt & pepper. Toss the dressing with the beans and Sultan-A's, then top with the yabbies.
Serve with coriander & parmesan cheese to taste.

101 WAYS TO COOK MARRON

101 WAYS TO COOK MARRON
RECIPE SUPPLIED BY:
BERNIE PEARL
THE TRUE MARRON 1.0.1

YABBY A LA BISQUE

10 WAYS TO COOK MARRON
RECIPE SUPPLIED BY
ADAM PURDY
THE TRUE MARRON T.C.1

INGREDIENTS
10 cooked large yabbies.
2 tbsp olive oil.
1 French shallot, finely sliced.
½ cup finely diced fennel.
Button mushrooms.
2 sprigs thyme.
1 bay leaf.
1 tbsp tomato paste.
2 tsp plain flour.
3 tomatoes, diced.
20ml cognac.
80ml white wine.
250ml (1 cup) yabby stock.
2 tbsp thin cream.
Pinch of cayenne pepper.
Juice of ½ lemon.
1 garlic clove, finely chopped.
Salt.
Freshly ground black pepper.
2 tbsp finely sliced chives.

METHOD
Detach the yabby heads from the body and peel the tails. Reserve the heads and shells and refrigerate the tails.

Heat the oil in a large cast-iron pan over high heat. When very hot, add the yabby heads and tail shells and stir for 2-3 minutes or until the shells change colour. Add the shallot, fennel, thyme and bay leaf and stir well.

Add the tomato paste and flour and stir well. Stir in the cognac, wine and stock, then add the diced tomatoes.

Reduce the heat to medium-low and simmer for 20 minutes.

Stir in the cream, cayenne pepper and lemon juice and cook for a further 5 minutes.

Strain the yabby sauce through a fine strainer into a clean saucepan, pressing on the shells firmly to extract as much flavour as possible.

To serve, gently reheat the yabby tails in the sauce and season to taste with salt and pepper. Stir in the garlic.

Ladle into deep soup plates and sprinkle with chives.

ONE 'SUPER' YABBY SHOULD DO IT?

OH! FANCY! I'LL BE SURE TO GIVE THIS ONE A GO!

101 WAYS TO COOK MARRON

YABBY & SAMPHIRE STIR FRIED NOODLES

INGREDIENTS
200g thin egg noodles.
16-20 raw large yabbies.
3 tbsp vegetable oil.
2 cloves of garlic.
50g of samphire or small handful.
1 tbsp root ginger, sliced finely.
1 strip cut carrot.
1/4 pineapple pieces.
2 tbsp soy sauce.
50g of snow peas.
50g of bean sprouts.
Handful of coriander.

METHOD
If you're like me, you'll follow the instructions on the fried noodles when you buy them. ;)
Bring a pot of water with a few pinches of salt to the boil and cook the noodles until al dente (gotta keep the fancy folk happy with the lingo) and drain well.
Preheat your grill on high.
Spread the yabbies out on a grilling tray, grilling for a few minutes each side until done. Heat the oil in a large wok and fry the ginger and garlic prior to adding the other ingredients.
Allow the heat to transfer through all the vegies, but still keep that good crunch.
Serve the noodles in a warm bowl with the yabbies and bits of coriander on the side.

SAMPHIRE - BEACH COOKING
Southern Australia's bush asparagus is a native succulent. Woody at the base and with many branches, it grows freely on many of southern Australia's salty flats. Samphire is considered best for use in summer when the fleshy leaves are bright green and aromatic. Though it can be eaten raw, samphire, like asparagus, is delicious lightly steamed and served with butter and makes a great accompaniment to fish and crayfish. The main thing to consider when cooking samphire is to rinse it thoroughly to remove any grit and excess salt, unless you like that kind of thing of course.

101 WAYS TO COOK MARRON

> LITTLE MARRON STIR-FRY WE HAD THIS PAST SEASON.
> SERVED WITH A SIDE OF HOME-MADE GARLIC BREAD. THE LITTLE COOK POTS ALMOST KEPT IT TOO HOT TO EAT.
> - MICK STANLEY

CRAY-Z IS AS CRAY-Z DOES
THE TRUE MARRON 1.0.1

Adam T Purdy

CHEESY MAZZ & MUSTARD SANGA

INGREDIENTS
1 marron tail per sandwich.
4 slices of preffered bread.
2 tbsp of butter.
150g of cheese.
1 thin sliced tomato.
3 tbsp créme fraiche.
2 tsp wholegrain mustard.
2 tsp chopped chives.

METHOD
Preheat sandwich press.
Butter both sides of the bread to get that golden toasted sandwich look.
Top two pieces with cheese, tomato slices and sliced marron tail.
Mix whole mustard, créme fraiche and chives and spread it over the other two slices.
Close the sangas and put them on the sandwich press.
Toast for 4 minutes or until the cheese has melted and the toast is golden.

MARRON CABAPPLE SALAD READY TO GO!

INGREDIENTS
150g of pre-cooked marron tail.
1 juiced lemon.
4 tbsp olive oil.
1 tsp crushed coriander seeds.
1/2 shredded red cabbage.
1 cored and finely sliced apple.

METHOD
Put the lemon juice, sliced marron tail, olive oil, coriander seeds and cabbage into a large bowl and mix it all together.
Let it stand for 10 minutes to soften the cabbage before adding the sliced apple.

SWEET CHILLI 4 MACON & BROCCOLI SALAD

INGREDIENTS
150g marron tail.
4 rashers of bacon.
1 head of broccoli florets.
3 tbsp olive oil.
1 tsp of dijon mustard.
1 tsp '**BEE JUICE**'.
1 tbsp balsamic vinegar.
Parmesan cheese to taste.

METHOD
Heat 1 tbsp of oil in a pan, fry the bacon and marron tail for 3 minutes on each side.
Get some salted boiling water and blanch the broccoli for 5 minutes or until they are tender. Drain when ready.
While the marron, bacon and broccoli is cooking, whisk the honey, mustard and vinegar with a pinch of salt the incorporate the rest of the oil.
Toss the drained broccoli with the dressing and divide between the two plates. Lay the bacon rashers on the top and sprinkle with your desired amount of parmesan cheese.

DEEP FRIED MARRON TAIL ROLLS

INGREDIENTS
BEER BATTER
To one cup of plain flour & half a cup of cornflour.
Add salt and ground white pepper.
Add enough 'cold' beer to make a nice stiff batter.
Dip pieces into beer batter and fry until golden brown.
Cut up a long fresh roll, & add fresh lettuce.

METHOD
Slice your tails into bite sizes pieces.
Put some sunflower oil into a pot.
Fry until floating (3-5mins).

DRESSING
3x tbsp of Worcestershire sauce.
3 x tbsp of bbq sauce.
4 x tbsp of egg mayonnaise.
Pepper.
Lemon juice to taste.

**COMBINE IN A BOWL AND STIR WELL.
GOOD FOR THE MORNING AFTER A BIG NIGHT.**

IT'S EASY AS!
1. PLACE MARRON PIECES ON THE ROLL
2. ADD YOUR DRESSING
3. EAT WHILE THE MARRON IS STILL HOT!
ENJOY!

NUTTY MACON & SHROOMS

Recipe supplied by: BLAZE PEARL – THE TRUE MARRON T.O.T

INGREDIENTS
200g marron tails uncooked.
3 sliced rashers of bacon.
200g mixed wild mushrooms
(Wood blewits, cepes & shiitake).
100g whole cooked & peeled chestnuts.
1 tbsp olive oil.
2 Finely chopped shallots.
1 tbsp of butter.
1 clove of crushed garlic.
1 tbsp chopped flat leaf parsley.

METHOD
If fresh picking the mushrooms, brush away any soil with a brush. Cut larger mushroom into smaller bite-sized bits.
Heat the olive oil in a large pan and fry the shallot, marron and bacon for 5 minutes. Add the mushies to the pan with the butter, season with salt & pepper, stir occasionlly for 10 minutes. When the mushroom liquid has evaporated and the mushrooms start to colour, add parsley, chestnuts and garlic and allow to set for a few minutes prior to serving.

MAZZ & THE RED HOT CHILLI PEPPERS

Recipe supplied by: PEPPY RINGBURNER – MARRON T.O.T

INGREDIENTS
2 little gem lettuces, separate leaves.
200g precooked marron tail.
1 diced red pepper.
1/2 red onion.
Handful of olives.
1 tbsp chopped basil.
4 tbsp olive oil.
2 hard-boiled eggs.

METHOD
Arrange the lettuce leaves on the serving plates and arrange the marron, peppers, onion and olives on the top.
Scatter the chopped basil and cover with olive oil.

GARNISH EACH PLATE WITH HALF A BOILED EGG.

CAMPFIRE GOOGIE MUSSELS & MARRON TAIL

INGREDIENTS
5 lbs fresh mussels.
2 lbs fresh marron tail.
10 cloves garlic, roughly chopped.
1 red onion, diced.
2 stalks leeks, chopped.
3 tbsp pesto sauce.
A couple of **GOOGIES** (beer can).
2 tbsp butter.

METHOD
First things first, make sure your heat source is nice and hot.
If you are cooking over a campfire ensure that your coals are red hot and throwing off some really nice heat.
Add in the butter and allow to melt. Once butter is melted toss in leeks, onions, garlic and allow them to soften and brown slightly. Mix in the pesto.
Add the mussels and marron into the pot and using your hands or large slotted spoon, toss to ensure all of the mussels are coated in the pesto mixture. Now add in the beer.
One beer is added, place top on pot and allow the mussels to steam and cook. Check in every 3-5 minutes and give everything a good stir, bringing the mussels that are on bottom to the top.
Let mussels cook for 8-10 minutes. I personally like my mussels left in a bit longer than normally recommended to avoid the sliminess you can sometimes get with undercooked mussels.
Once mussels look completed remove from heat and serve immediately in pot with fresh sour dough or crispy french fries. This is my twist to the authentic way.

101 WAYS TO COOK MARRON PICTURE SUPPLIED BY JUSTIN PERONI — THE TRUE MARRON T.O.1

101 WAYS TO COOK MARRON RECIPE SUPPLIED BY BLAZE PEARL — THE TRUE MARRON T.O.1

YABBY & PINEAPPLE STIR-FRY

INGREDIENTS
200g of peeled raw yabbies.
3 tbsp of vegetable oil.
2 cloves of thinly sliced garlic.
1 tbsp thinly sliced root ginger.
300g pineapple rings, dried & halved.
1 tbsp caster sugar.
1 tbsp light soy sauce.
2 tbsp rice wine.
Chives, inch long lengths.

METHOD
Heat oil in a large wok and fry the ginger and garlic. Quickly add the yabbies and pineapple and stir-fry for 3 minutes or until yabbies turn opaque. Combine the rice wine, soy sauce and sugar together before adding it to the wok. Stir-fry for 2 minutes then serve.

CHUCK THOSE CHIVES ON!

NO MORE CRAY-Z HEAD.
Crayfish help in the development of bones. They have high levels of minerals such as: Calcium and Magnesium. Both are essential in the development of bones and hair growth. The Omega-3 found in crayfish is great for kids and doesn't taste as horrible as the liquid capsules. Omega-3 also helps with motor skills in children and have a great impact on those suffering from depression.
IF ONLY WE COULD GET A MEDICAL CERTIFICATE TO GO MARRONING.

101 WAYS TO COOK MARRON

BUTTONED UP MARRON IN A BLANKET

Recipe supplied by **HEINRICH** — THE TRUE MARRON T.O.T

INGREDIENTS
Precooked marron tails.
6 thin slices of bacon, halved.
12 button mushrooms.
Cut chillies to fit in base of the mushies.
4 tbsp of **ROSE INFUSED** honey.
1 lime, cut into wedges.
Coriander to garnish.

METHOD
Put wooden skewers in a bowl of cold water for 20 minutes.
Preheat the grill until it is hot.
Wrap the marron tails in bacon.
Stuff the 'as-close to shape' as you can chilli into the bases of the button mushrooms prior to threading the button mushrooms on each end.
(Hopefully the pepper will have a rich kick with the infused honey).
Drizzle each kebab with a generous amount of honey.
Grill kebabs for 5 minutes on each side or until golden brown.
Serve with lime and coriander.

101 WAYS TO COOK MARRON

MAZZ ON A STICK

Recipe supplied by **SHANTEL BERGROTH** — THE TRUE MARRON T.O.T

WE ONLY NEED 10 MINS

INGREDIENTS
Marron.
Hot salami.
Grapes.
Cheese.
Kebab sticks.

METHOD
Slice ingredients, on a kebab stick add marron, hot salami cheese, grape.

REPEAT PROCESS TIL ALL GONE!

PIRI-PIRI MARRON ON A STICK

Recipe supplied by BLAZE PEARL, The True Marron 1.0.1

INGREDIENTS
450g of marron tails, peeled with tails left intact.
3 cloves of crushed garlic.
1 tbsp fine chopped flat leaf parsley.
1/2 tsp smoked paprika.
2 tbsp olive oil.
2 red peppers, chunks.
Lemon wedges.
Crusty bread to serve.

METHOD
Mix the chilli, garlic, paprika and oil together with a pinch of salt.
Put the marron tails and chunks of pepper into a freezer bag, add the piri-piri marinade.
Tie a knot in the bag and slowly massage it in.
Really get the flavours through the flesh.. Leave it for 30 minutes while you cool down.
Soak yourself & skewers in cold water for at least 20 minutes.
Preheat the grill.
Put the marron tails & peppers onto the skewers and grill for a quick 2 minutes on each side or until flesh is cooked through.
Ready to eat served with lemon wedges and crusty bread.

Picture supplied by GREG MATTHEWS, The True Marron 1.0.1

MAZZ'Z BALLS

Recipe supplied by CLOVE R. LIC, The True Marron 1.0.1

INGREDIENTS
400g precooked marron tails.
1 crushed clove of garlic.
Black olives, to taste.
5 spring onion, chopped to half inch.
1/2 tsp ground cinnamon.
1/2 tsp coriander.
1 tsp cumin.
2-3 ltrs of sunflower oil or your preffered frying oil.

GOES WELL WITH A LIGHT SALAD & A GLASS OF WINE.

METHOD
Put all ingredients into a blender (besides the 2-3ltrs of oil) and whisk it into a gooey paste... Is he watching?
Heat the oil in a deep fryer to a maximum of 180°C.
Glare directly at your man while you use an icecream scoop to shape the balls and drop them straight into the boiling oil.
Fry the marron balls for 3-5 minutes, depending on shape & size. Should be golden brown. a knife should come out clean when stabbed.
Line a bowl with kitchen paper to absorb any excess oil... and the tears on your husbands face.
Sprinkle with a little sea salt.

LIME, CAPSICUM, SILVERBEET & LEMON. SIMPLE BUT YUMMY! MARK CUZENS
CRAY-Z IS AS CRAY-Z DOES
THE TRUE MARRON
1.0.1
Adam T Purdy

MARRON, COCONUT AND LIME LEAF STICKS

INGREDIENTS
As many marron tails as you like!
Frozen lime leaves.
1 tbsp vegetable oil.
Grated creamed coconut.

METHOD
Heat the BBQ until smoking hot. Thread the marron tail and lime leaves onto metal skewers.
Stir the oil into the creamed coconut, then drop the skewers in the mixture or use a dressing brush.
Cook the skewers for 2-3 minutes on each side or until cooked through.

I TOLD YOU! EVERYONE LOVES ME!

A TIMELESS TRUFFLE, MARRON & KIPFLER SALAD

INGREDIENTS
1 350g marron.
4 small kipfler potatoes.
Handfull of Mache* leaves.
5 slices Timeless Black Truffle.
5 chervil sprigs.
3 slices crisp pancetta.
1 tbs chardonnay vinegar.
4 tbs Bookalaam Olive Oil.
1 tbs djon mustard.
A pinch of sea salt.
1 twist of the peppermill.

METHOD
Cook the marron in a court bouillon for 5 mins refreshin ice water, peel and slice into 5 disks.
Cook the kipflers in well salted water until al dente. Peel while still warm.
Combine vinegar, mustard, oil and seasoning for dressing.
Slice potatoes into neat disks, reheat.
Add remaining ingredients dress liberally.
Not all the dressing will be required. Toss carefully and arrange nicely in a shallow bowl.

*MACHE LEAVES ARE A COLD SALAD GREEN.. IT'S FANCY!

TOSSED YABBY SALAD

INGREDIENTS
1kg live yabbies.
2 cups wild or baby rocket.
¼ cup extra virgin olive oil.
1½ tablespoons lemon juice.
2 tomatoes, peeled, seeded and finely diced.
2 tablespoons finely chopped basil.
Salt flakes and freshly ground black pepper, to taste.

METHOD
Bring a large saucepan of salted water to the boil.
Add the yabbies and simmer for 3-4 minutes, until the shells turn orange. Drain and set-aside until just cool enough to handle.
Twist off the yabbies claws and crack open to remove the meat.
Twist off and discard the heads. Insert kitchen scissors into the base of the tail and cut along the centre of the underside of the shell.
Carefully prise open the shell and remove the tail meat.
Discard shells.
Slice the tail meat in half lengthways and devein.
Divide rocket between 4 plates and top with yabby meat.
Combine olive oil, lemon juice, tomato, basil, salt and pepper and mix well.

SYDNEY SEAFOOD SCHOOL
sydney fish market

> IF YOU ARE STRUGGLING WITH THAT KILO OF YABBIES? I'LL BE MORE THAN HAPPY TO GIVE YOU A FIN?

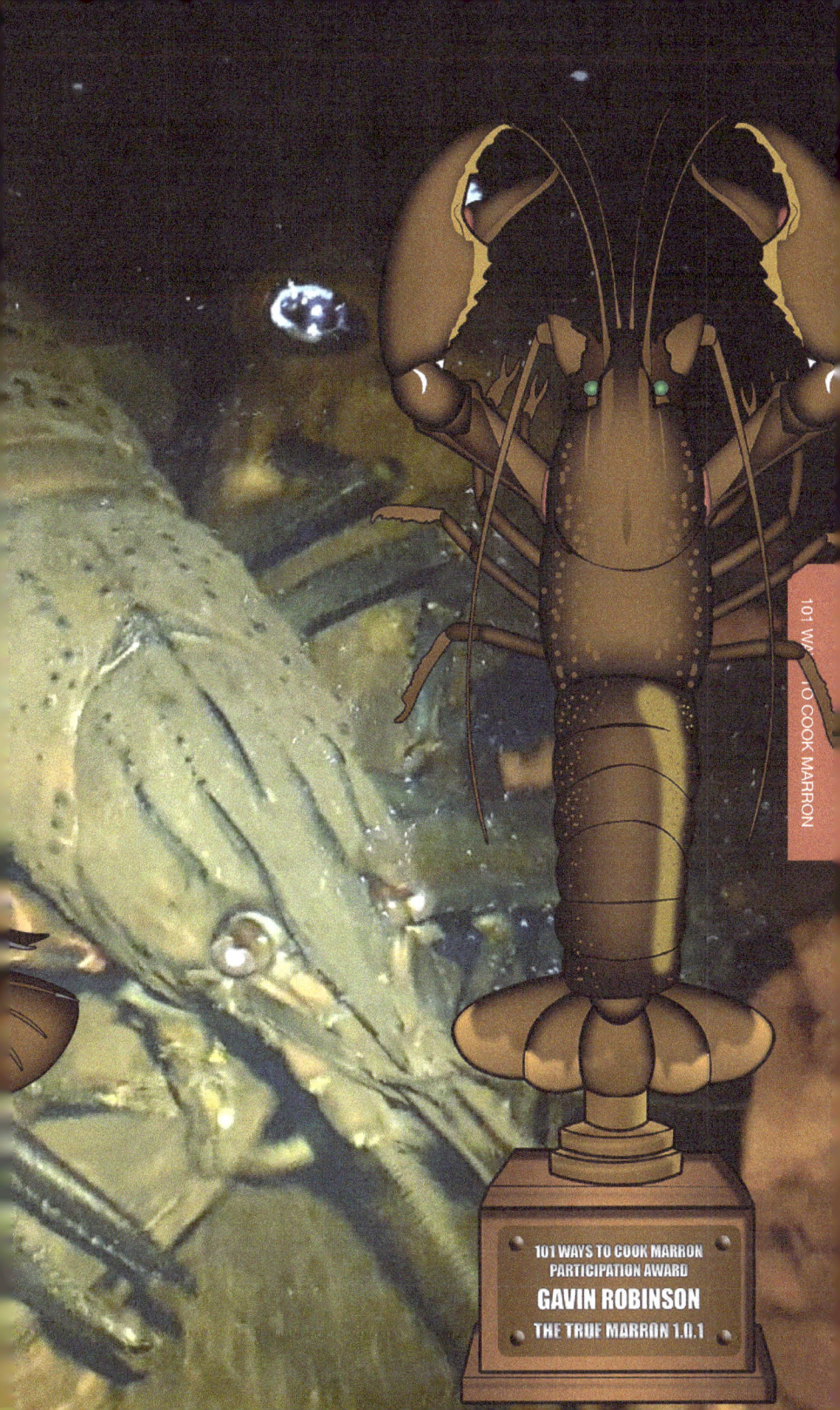

MARRON, TRUFFLE & ASPARAGUS SALAD

INGREDIENTS
300gm marron.
400g kipfler potatoes.
500g blanched asparagus.
60g fresh black truffle, thinly sliced.
200g curly endive, washed.
2 punnets lamb's lettuce (mâche), trimmed and washed.
1 tbsp chervil leaves.

TRUFFLE DRESSING
1 tbsp aged red wine vinegar.
2 tbsp dry white wine.
10g fresh black truffle, finely chopped.
125 ml (½ cup),
Bookalaam olive oil.

METHOD
Boil marron, remove meat and cut into thirds lengthways.
Peel, boil and thickly sliced Kipfler potatoes.
For truffle dressing, combine vinegar, wine and truffle in a bowl and whisk to combine.
Add olive oil in a steady stream, whisking until incorporated.
Season to taste with sea salt and freshly ground white pepper.
For salad, divide ingredients between serving bowls, drizzle with truffle dressing and toss gently to combine.

SERVE IMMEDIATELY

"MY FRIENDS & I WOULD MAKE A GOOD SIDE-DISH FOR THIS ONE,"

NOTES:

101 WAYS TO COOK MARRON

BOOKALAAM MARRON WITH TRUFFLE & MANGO SALAD

INGREDIENTS
FOR THE DRESSING
Nam jim dressing.
2 cloves garlic.
4 coriander roots and stem.
Pinch of salt.
3 red chillies, deseeded & chopped.
60g grated palm sugar.
3 tbsp fish sauce.
Juice from 2 limes.
1 shallot, finely sliced.

MARRON & SALAD
4 large live marron.
Bookalaam Olive Oil.
2 green mangoes.
3 slices of Timeless Hill Black Truffle.
1 red chilli finely, sliced.
4 mint leaves, finely sliced.
Shaved Pink Salt.
Thai basil leaves.
Coriander leaves.

METHOD
FOR THE DRESSING
In a mortar and pestle crush the garlic and coriander root with salt until you have a paste. Add the chopped red chillies and crush until lightly broken up.
Add the fish sauce, lime juice and sliced shallots.

CHECKING THE FLAVOUR; You should be able to ignite all the tastes, salty, sweet, sour and heat from the peppers, adjust accordingly.

FOR THE MARRON
Put live marron in freezer for 20 minutes (this will render them unconscious), then cut through the middle with a sharp knife (pierce the keel first.
Pull out the intestinal tract. Sprinkle with Shaved Pink Salt and Bookalaam Olive Oil. Put flesh down onto very hot, clean barbecue and cook for five minutes. Turn and cook until the flesh has turned opaque and pulls away from the shell.

FOR THE SALAD
Peel the mangoes then slice thinly and stir through the dressing along with the black truffle, red chilli and herbs.
Pile a small handful onto the plate next to the barbeced marron.
Drizzle with Bookalaam olive oil.

Serve immediately either in the shell or you can pull the meat out and serve tossed through the salad.

RECIPE SUPPLIED BY:
ADAM PURDY

PICTURE SUPPLIED BY:
BOOKALAAM OLIVE GROVE

ARE OUR NATURAL SPRINGS THE ANSWER?

Natural springs like this one lead down to underground caverns. Some crayfish species may be still surving underneath their natural habitat. Locating a natural spring is always a good sign on crustaceans being in the area. Crayfish love sitting where the water can flow past them and allow them to eat with minimal energy. If you watch marron while the water is flowing and then turn off the water flow, the marron will go in the direction the water came from.

This piece of information has had me studying our aquifers and caves searching for signs of our regions Hairy Marron.

Is the answer to this species survival right under our feet? Time will tell. - Adam Purdy 2022

MARRON 'TORTURE'LLINI

IT'S OK! LITTLE GUY! I WON'T LET ANYONE HURT YOU!

INGREDIENTS
FOR THE PASTA
700g bakers flour.
1 tsp olive oil.
1/2 tsp salt.
2 large eggs.

FOR THE FILLING
2 Raw marron.
Salt.
Pepper.
Dill (not a **Dil**).
Whisked egg whites.
Drizzle of lactose free cream.

METHOD
FOR THE PASTA
Whisk the eggs into a wash.
Sieve the flour into a bowl and make a well in the centre.
Add a splash of olive oil & a pinch or two of salt.
Pour the whisked eggs into the well and gradually mix with either a blunt knife or your hands. When the dough has become a thick paste use your hands to knead in more of the flour.
It helps to put flour on your hands while you knead the dough to stop it sticking to the surface and to your hands, but be careful not to make the dough too dry.
Knead until well blended and the dough is soft and flexible.
Leave the pasta to rest for about an hour, covered and leave it.
You can sieve any leftover flour again and save this flour for rolling out the pasta.

FOR THE FILLING
Place your marron into a large pot of boiling salted water for 1½ minutes. Using tongs transfer marron to a large bowl of iced water. Once chilled, remove the claws and head. Crack open the marron tail and claw shells and remove the meat.
Mince the flesh from the Marron. Add a pinch of salt, pepper and a sprinkling of dill (not the **ENDANGERED DIL**).
For binding add a couple of egg whites and a drizzle of cream. Blend this all together.
Roll out the pasta into a long, wide strip about 2mm in thickness, when you see your hand through it, it is ready for the filling.
Using a cup or round cutter, make 4 circles of pasta around each mound of filling. Place teaspoons of the filling in a line down the centre of one of the strips then close the lids up.
To cook, bring a large pan of salted water to the boil and gently lower in the tortellini. Cook for about four minutes or until the pasta is soft but not floppy.

WHEN THE PASTA IS DONE, DRAIN IT & SERVE IMMEDIATELY

PADDOCK & POND ON A STICK WITH CHIPS

101 WAYS TO COOK MARRON
RECIPE SUPPLIED BY:
ADAM PURDY
THE TRUE MARRON T.U.T

INGREDIENTS
400g thin cut chips.
350g cubed sirloin steak.
250g cubed marron tail.
1 cubed green pepper.
1 cubed onion.
2 tbsp olive oil.
Cumin to taste.

SALADS TO SERVE

METHOD
Cook the sirloin steak in advance, but still warm for a quick reheat (medium rare to allow for further cooking)
Soak wooden skewers in a bowl of water for 20 minutes.
Preheat oven to 220°C
Spread the chips out on a baking tray spray with oil and coat with cumin
Cook for 10 minutes or until crunchy
Preheat your grill until hot.
Thread alternating chunks of meat, marron, onion and peppers until all chunks are used up... no waste ;)
Brush with oil and season with salt & pepper.
Grill the kebabs for 4 minutes on each side or until marron is cooked through.
Sprinkle the chips with salt & pepper and serve on a bed of salad.

101 WAYS TO COOK MARRON

CHECK OUT PAULA'S CHIVE & CHEESE SAUCE ON THE NEXT PAGE!

CHIVE & CHEESE SAUCE

INGREDIENTS
2-3 tablespoons butter.
Diced chives.
1 diced onions.
6-7 tablespoon plain flour.
2-3 cups milk.
1/2 cup grated cheese.
Splash Worcestershire sauce.
Splash olive oil.
Salt & Pepper.

METHOD
Amounts vary depending on amount of marron. Heat 3-4 tablespoon butter with splash of oil (oil stops the butter from burning). Add diced onions and cook till soft set aside in a bowl. Add more butter and oil melt then add plain flour whisk to a paste then slowly add milk (once you have amount of milk you are happy with put back on the heat) while still whisking add salt and pepper to taste, grated cheese, chives, Worcestershire sauce and lemon juice a couple of good splashes of both keep whisking until it comes up to the thickness you like (if not thick enough mix a little bit more of plain flour in a cup with little bit of water until smooth then add into mixture) take off the heat and pour over marron.

GARLIC & LEMON MARRON

INGREDIENTS
Marron
1-2 teaspoons garlic.
Squeezes lemon.
Butter.
Salt & Pepper.

METHOD
Blanch marron in boiling water for 2-3 mins, then take out peel and cut in half length ways. Heat 2- 4 teaspoons butter (depending on amount of marron) with a splash of oil once melted add as much garlic, salt and pepper as you like to suit your taste then put in marron and cook for a further two minutes turning constantly once cooked arrange on plate with white sauce.

YOU MIGHT KNOW MY GREAT GRAND FATHER PIG NUGENT?

THE DEHYDRATOR - DJOOL ARMY MAKER

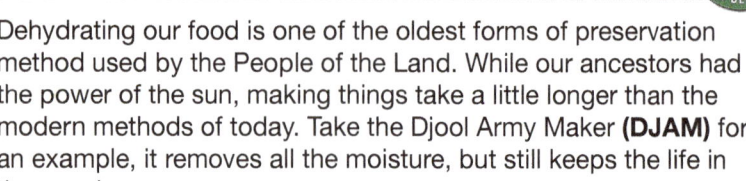

Dehydrating our food is one of the oldest forms of preservation method used by the People of the Land. While our ancestors had the power of the sun, making things take a little longer than the modern methods of today. Take the Djool Army Maker **(DJAM)** for an example, it removes all the moisture, but still keeps the life in the specimen.

Normally I used the **DJAM** to create my minions to do my dirty work, the Sultan A's, the Tom-inions and the Cap-C-YUMs. They sneak their way into recipes and absorb all the flavours they are mixed with. Works expecially well with most crayfish meals. I have noticed they go well on long hikes and don't take up as much room as their plumpy counterparts.

Almost anything can be dehydrated, some common food items made with dehydration include: Fruit leathers, soup mixes ie: dehydrated onions, carrots, mushrooms, peppers. Herbs dehydrated for a longer shelf life. Powdered lemon, lime, or orange peel used in teas, alcoholic beverages, among other things. You can dehydrate your own fruits, vegetables, herbs, and even Chef Macon can be done in your oven or quicker in the **DJAM**
Many dehydrated foods are available in stores as well, though watch out for added ingredients like sodium, sugar, or oils.
Just remember we get a lot of water from the food we eat.
If you are camping with a heap of dehydrated vegies and fruits remember to keep your liquids up through other avenues.
Staying hydrated aids in digestion, blood pressure management, joint health and flushing bacteria from your body. All a big **MUST** while out enjoying nature!

BERNIES DJAM EVIL PLAN

I have decided to share with you my plan. But first off, let me tell you how I get the most out of the rest of the team mates. I got them to pose for a group photo before I introduced them to the **DJAM**.

THE GRAPES - SULTAN A'S
My ultimate Minion, The Grapes are the plumpy version of my Sultan A's, the most versitile of the Djool Army. Making them is a little tricky, as I need to remove all moisture or moulds can form and ruin my end result. First off, I prick the grapes to allow all their liquids to drain as they make their way through the Dehydrator. I set the machine to 58°C for 18-45 hours. I can store my Sultan A's in their airtight glass storage device for a few years until needed.

THE CAPSICUMS - CAP-C-YUMS
These hollow heads, may find themselves heading to The Black Pearl Mortician Service if they can't get themselves into any recipes soon! Perhaps after drying them for 4 hours at 120°C, I should of put them in a containment cell with garlic and herbs. Covering them all in oil & letting it sit for a few weeks would of made them more enticing I suppose. If all else fails their **R.I.POWDER** would go well for stocks and added spice.

TOMATOES - TOM-INIONS
Making the Tom-inions is a little more hands on than some of the others. The tomatoes sugar rich juices can cause them to stick to the conveyor. I prick my full tomatoes for drainage and for 8-14 hours at 52°C, I get Ugh to stand there and give them a flip once in a while. My Minions are ready when they are dry & leathery. I have heard thinly slicing the tomato prior to running them through my machine, would of made drying and storage a little easier. Perhaps next time!

PEPPY AND THE RED HOT CHILLI PEPPERS
As much as I am grateful for Peppy bringing 'us' Pearls into the group. I will admit, I have thought about how he would benefit me as a member of the Djool Army. It would only take 8 to 12 hours to dry him in a dehydrator at 140°F. (I wonder if my dehydrator can go that high? Can yours?) I might need a furness to get those levels of heat? If all else fails I could hang him in the sun until he is completly dried. His way of adapting to every recipe is just what my Djool Army needs and I'll change the band name to 'Deep Purple' once he's out of the picture.

MORE OF BERNIES DJAM EVIL PLAN

THE FUN-GUYS
These guys like to stick together! I've learnt to ensure there is enough space between the Fun-Guys for airflow, they sweat lots! These stinky fellas get a good wash and let them dry off before we turn them. I find 3-8 hours at 55°C is enough to take the humour out of them. They should be brittle and break when dry. It's straight to our Mortician Service for the Roomies, they know too much! Their **R.I.Powder** will bring an earthy flavour to any campers meal.

THE CITRIC FAMILY
Ah!! The Citric Duo!! Limetta and I go way back, after all we have accomplished it would be a shame to have her join Pucka on a trip through the **DJAM**. But her flavour is a compliment to any dish, so we will just have to see if the plan goes through won't we!
If not slicing them and running them through the **DJAM**, shouldn't take longer than 6-8 hours at 58°C. Limetta would make a good Djool Squad member, I've often thought of her and Oranges dipped in chocolate.. Hmmm.

CHRIS P. BACON & CO.
This big boy needs to be cut down to size depending on your **DJAM**. 6-7 hours at 62°C does well for 1" long strips. Ugh finds blotting the oil droplets that form on the meat with paper towels quite soothing. When I have Chris P. Bacon, I'll break him into even smaller pieces for use in recipes. Another great candidate for The Mortician Service. You could even use his **R.I.POWDER** in a Marron omelette.

DANY D. & THE 'HERB'STORIANS
Luckily for me I haven't forgotten the benefits of the Lion Family and their friends. Problem is, their flower heads, leaves and roots all need to be **DJAM'ED** at different heats. Flower heads and leaves are dried at 35°C, the roots are done at 50°C. Either way as part of my Djool Squad, they make a great cup of tea and the roots a great coffee.
THE R.I.POWDER from The Lion Family and the other 'Herb'storians come each with either own medicinal benefits too. But I don't have time to tell you about that!..

WHEN IT ALL COMES DOWN TO THE

IT'S MAZZ I'M AFTER,
HE'S GOING STRAIGHT FOR SHREDDER WASTE!

MAZZ'S PART OF BERNIES DJAM EVIL PLAN

"My plan for our Head judge, Mr Mazz C. Cainii himself! Is to kidnap him. Yep! That's it! End of story. BAHAHA, Yeah Right! Let me tell you what I have in mind!

With the help of a good friend of mine, I'll make my very own brand of Marron Salt. Surely I will win all the trophies with this clever idea! First off, Mazz wont fit in the **DJAM**. So I've had to think of a few other options:

OPTION 1: PURCHASE A FURNESS.

Apparently '**HUMANS**' call them '**OVENS**' according to Eli. But once I get one, I'll Preheat it to 250°C set on Fan Bake, I'll chuck him straight on the racks and bake him for 25 minutes. Ugh will get his brush out and dab him with vegetable, sunflower or some other odourless oil. Bookalaam Olive grove has a range 'Pur'fect for this. I'll have Ugh watch him while he takes another run through the Furness for 15 minutes. This will make sure he is completely dried but not charred. We'll take him out and let him cool down completely before heading to the Mortuary. A few good wizzes in the blender and 'Hey Pesto!' I have my Marron Salt!

Before I tell you the second option, this is how I plan to use our Mr M. C. Cainii variety shredder waste. **MAZZ R.I.POWDER** is used as a seasoning to give flavour to soups, stews, sauces, and other dishes that require an aromatic hint of flavour. It is chocker block full of vitamin B, protein, iron, zinc, and amino acids, making it a healthy addition to any dish. Mazz Salt is a better and healthier option than Chickened Salt and is beneficial for our teeth.. and at least this **ACTUALLY** has **MARRON** in it!.

BERNIE GOES OLD SCHOOL ON MAZZ

MY MUM USES ONE! SILLY PEARL!

Apparently a Furness or as Eli says, '**AN OVEN**' is pretty expensive so...

MY PLAN B!

STEP 1. This means waiting for Summer or at least a week of good weather. Once I know I have the right gap in the weather, I'll grab the largest pot I can find to fit him in.. Hmmm, Perhaps I could do it with a yabbies too, the more the merrier I say! I just need enough water to make sure they are all covered by the water.

STEP 2. The trick is, to use double the amount of salt you would use for boiling crayfish normally. If I wait for the water to boil, drop them in head first they should only take 10-15 minutes to turn red and be ready to be drained.
I'll keep the drained liquid, freeze it if I have too. It can be used for gravies or as a stock for soups and stews, another good way for me to win this competition.
I call it '**BEETLE' JUICE**, I'll have people chanting it in mirrors before you know it!

STEP 3. Next I'll need a wooden table or a large grilled surface big enough to lay this 2kg Marron on. If I was to do it to yabbies, I would line them up in army formation, this will stop the overcrowding on my chosen surface.

STEP 4. Now Ugh gets the fun of turning Mazz every 3-4 hours this will ensure he dries on both sides. Wouldn't be so boring for him doing it with the Yabbies I suppose?

STEP 5. Blaze and Ugh are to be on watch every evening. The Shells are to be covered at dusk and bought into the base. Night air definatley puts a '**DAMPENER**' on this venture with the moisture it brings in with it. So they are to be on close watch. Don't want to poison anyone now do we?

101 WAYS TO COOK MARRON

HERCULES COULDN'T TAKE THIS BEATING!

STEP 6. This process will go on for 3-4 days. I must make a note to make sure they are completely dry. The head and shells should of pulled away from the body by now though. This should be a good sign they are done.

STEP 7. NOW THE FUN PART! I'll get the shells, put them in a sack or pillowcase and beat into it! Thats right! I'll get Nannas' rolling pin, baseball bat or whatever feels good in the hand and **'GO OLD SCHOOL ON IT'**. Even go as far as having a few good swings at a wall with it. **HECK!** Once I'm confident the shells have all been broken up. It's back onto the table to separate the grit. I have a fan that should do the trick, but leaving them on the table outside with a mild wind will blow all the grit away just as well.

STEP 8. Clear the schedule for the Black Pearl Morticuary Feed the shell through the Shredder Waste Service.

STEP 9. Store in our custom made, **GLASS URN DJOOL WASTE** Containment Vessels.

STEP 10. Win this competition with my Ultimate dish!!

STEP 11. Lauch **'MY'** Marron Salt on the World Market.

101 WAYS TO COOK MARRON

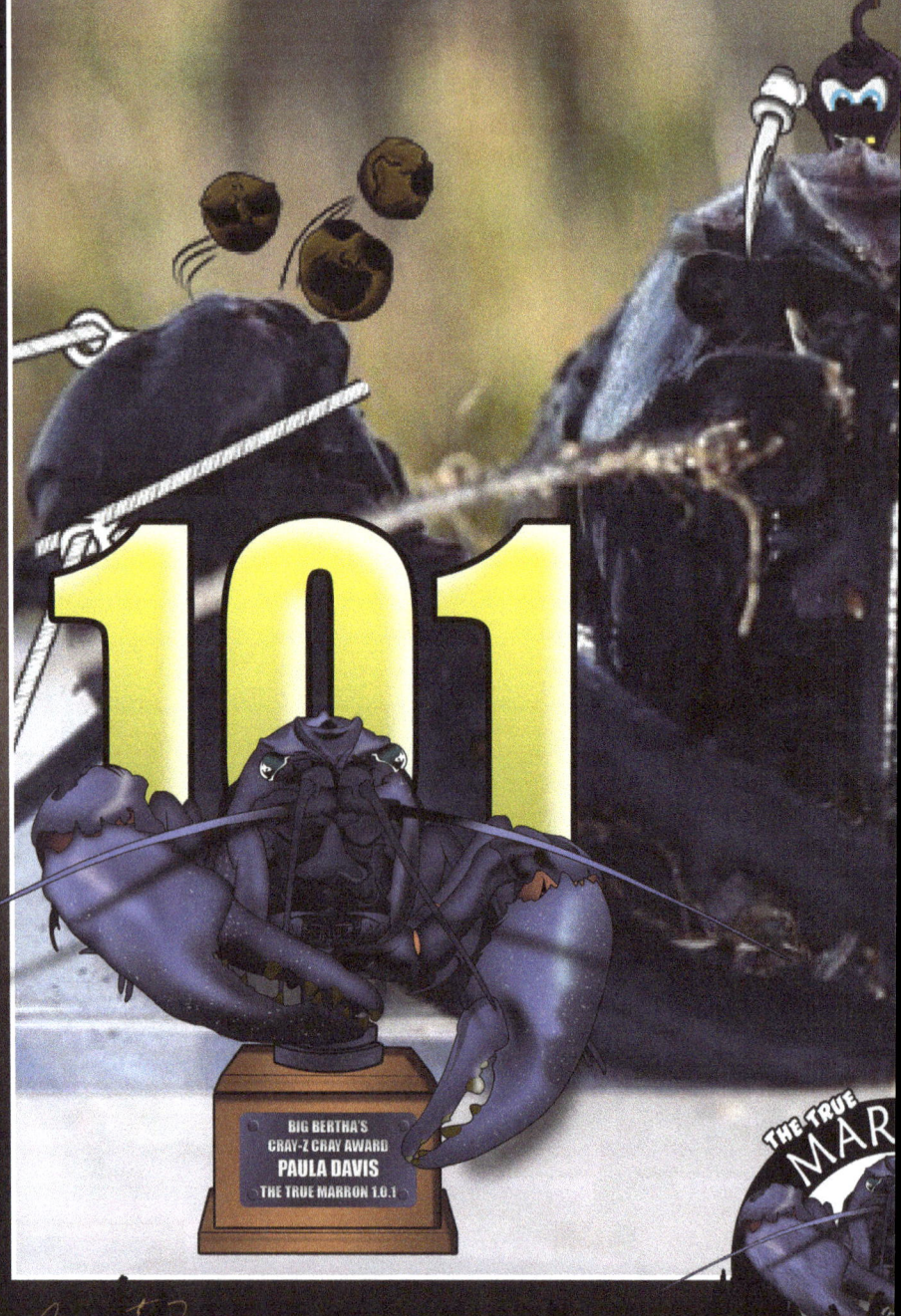

101 WAYS TO COOK MARRON

CHAR-GRILLED CLOVE WITH CAP-C-YUM & MAZZ

INGREDIENTS
Half a dozen marron, big ones.
200g packet of fettuccine.
A big ass red onion.
Lots of garlic.
A cask of white wine.
500ml thickened cream.
A jar of semi sun dried tomatoes.
2 red capsicums.
Zest of a lemon, finely grated.
A bunch of basil.
Handfuls of baby spinach.
Pine nuts, toasted.
Finely grated pecorino, basil leaves.
lemon wedges to serve.

THIS ONE NEEDS A HANDFUL OF DRIED CHILLI FLAKES CHUCKED IN!

METHOD
First, char-grill the capsicum by plonking them on the stove, right on the burner, really burn'em all over. When black and crusty looking all over remove to a bowl, cover with cling wrap and allow to sweat for a while (have a beer, get stuck into the 'goon').
The charred skin should rub of easily now, a few black bits are ok, remove stem, pith and seeds, cut into strips and place in a bowl with sundried tomatoes, mix'em round, walk away.
Put a large pot of salted water on high heat and bring to the boil. Put 2 or 3 marron in and pop the lid back on for 30 sec to a minute. This will seal and part cook the marron making them easy to shell. Move to an ice bath and cook the rest. Once cool enough to handle remove head, shell and 'poo tube' (dam water is generally muddy so this has to be done) and cut into chunks. Cook pasta al dente according to packet directions, strain and put aside.
Get a big pan hot, add a splash of oil and some butter and quickly fry the marron chunks just for a bit of colour, remove and put aside. Finely dice onion, add to pan with a bit more oil if needed followed by 4-5 finely chopped or crushed garlic cloves. Give that a stir then in with a heap of wine, at least half a litre. A bottle of wine will do it, throw a bit down the gullet as well. Boil for a bit to get rid of the booze, (now it's kid friendly) add the cream and turn the heat to medium. After the sauce has thickened slightly, go to town with (fold in) the rest of the ingredients. Add more cream if necessary, Garnish with basil leaves, pecorino and lemon wedges.

CHILLI MARRON SPAGHETTI

INGREDIENTS
375g marinated mussels (drain juice).
500g yabbies.
300g marron.
3 tins of diced tomato.
2 tbls of tomato paste.
3 cloves of garlic.
1 red onion.
1 tbls of chilli.
Pinch of chilli flakes.
Pinch of cracked pepper.
1 tsp of butter.
500g of spaghetti.
Cup of grated cheese.
Wedge of lemon.
Sprig of parsley.

METHOD
In a small pot combine diced tomato and tomato paste with half a cup of water. Simmer for 10 min while putting spaghetti on to cook 8-12 min in frying pan, sauté onions add garlic, chilli, chilli flakes, cracked pepper.
Stir fry in yabbies and marron.
Fry for 1 min, add mussels and marron, fry for 2min.
Combine ingredients with the sauce and simmer for 3 mins drain spaghetti, add the sauce to the spaghetti.
Lightly toss together sprinkle with cheese garnish with a sprig of parsley and a wedge of lemon.

GO NUTS! AND LOAD UP ON THE CHEESINESS!

101 WAYS TO COOK MARRON

MARRON PARMY

INGREDIENTS
425g tuna in brine.
300-500g prawns.
300-500g of marron.
500g spaghetti.
200g diced bacon.
600ml thickened cream.
1 cup tasty cheese.
50g of parmesan cheese.
1 tbls of black pepper.
Pinch of chilli flakes.

METHOD
Put pasta on to cook 10-12 mins. Fry bacon add prawns and marron. Fry for 2 mins. Add tuna, cream, cheese, pepper & chilli flakes. Let simmer for 10-12 mins before you drain pasta and add it to the sauce, lightly mix. Serve with extra grated cheese if desired.

BEST SERVED WITH WHITE WINE OR LIGHT BEER.

WESTERN COMMON REED - WONDER REED

Our Western Common Reed or it's latin name *Phragmites australis*.. Seriously? who names these things?? (Frag-Mites??) just wow! I just 'froogled' **WONDER REED** and it came out with *Mirantibus arundo* (Myra- Anti-Bus I-Run-Dough), so either ways its latin name is doomed.. a little more energetic, but still doomed.
So Wonder Reed it is, nothing, fancy!

BUT BOY IS THIS PLANT VERSITILE!
The People of the Land have been using common reed well before a western medicine book came into existance. They would use the stems to build walls, thatched rooves, fences and to even insulate their homes. The ones with these skills, would sit around plaiting baskets, mats and making clothing for themselves and others. That all sounds great, but you can't eat any of that!
So you'd be surprised to know the sugar extracted from the stems and shoots, has a subtle liquorice sweet-like taste, that is great for chewing raw while walking the trails. You can also make your own bush lollies by boiling down the stems. You do this by boiling the stems in warm water, then reducing the mix with evaporation to obtain a sugary gum. This can be rolled into balls and sucked on like a boiled lollie. The seeds from the catstail can be ground into a powder and used as a form of flour for a beautiful bush damper.
The young lighter colour shoots can be eaten raw or cooked, they go great in salads raw and have a great flavour to add to any marron of fish recipe.
Now one of my favourite parts are the roots.
These can be eaten raw or cooked, in nearly any style you can cook potatoes. They make incredible fried chips and baked in oil with native herbs, really brings you back to the land.
I have also come across recipes where the People of the Land would grind the dried roots into a powder and eat it as a form of porridge which could of been baked to make a hard biscuit.
This would be a great plant to keep an eye out for when stranded on the side of the road or bogged in that mud puddle you just had to play in. It might just help keep you moving as a need for survial.

**WE RESPECT THE PEOPLE
OF THE LAND & THEIR TRADITIONS.**

'THE NATIVES DIG THE ROOTS UP, CLEAN THEM, ROAST THEM, AND THEN POUND THEM INTO A MASS, WHICH, WHEN KNEADED AND MADE INTO A CAKE, TASTES LIKE FLOUR NOT SEPARATED FROM THE BRAN.' (MOORE 1842)

101 WAYS TO COOK MARRON

"THAT'S PURDY!"

101 WAYS TO COOK MARRON
WE'RE NOT CRAY-CIST AWARD
MARK CUZENS
THE TRUE MARRON 1.0.1

MARRON & DUTCH CHEESE PASTA

I'LL BE SURE TO PUT EXTRA CHEESE ON MINE! YUM!

SURE YOU ARE MAZZ! YOU KNOW YOU CANNOT HAVE MILK!

INGREDIENTS
1 cup of tasty cheese.
4 tbls of cream cheese spread.
100 grams of herb and garlic feta.
600ml of thickened cream.
Bacon.
Marron.
3 thin slices of smoked dutch cheese.
500 grams of spaghetti.

METHOD
Put spaghetti on to cook 10-12 mins.
Fry bacon till almost crispy,
Add marron fry for 2 mins.
Add cream, bring to a slow boil,
Add all 4 cheeses and
simmer for 12-15 minutes.
Drain pasta & add to your sauce.
Light stir and serve.

CSIRAX - YABBY DABBA DOO'S 'CELERY'ITY JUDGE

Csirax and Mazz became friend at the beginning of the competition when Mazz was using his **'TIN CAN TELEPHONE'** looking for Sponsors for the:
101 WAYS TO COOK MARRON - RECIPE COMPETITION.
Csirax, Jamie and the Crew at Yabby Dabba Doo N.S.W, dedicate a lot of their time to the passing down of knowledge to our younger generations about the farming side of the **CRAY-Z** Industry.
Due to the hard work and effort with dealing with the kids, Mazz thought he would be a great **'CELERY'ITY JUDGE** for the show.
The **'HUMANS'** using it for their show had moved out and we could use it only if we cleaned up after the vandals who turned it into a **'RATS NEST'** crating their own version of the show. Once we explained the problem to Csirax, he took off his glasses, put on his cape and had the area imaculate in no time! We managed to produce a show with spending little-to-no **NIPCOINS**.
Csirax is a **SUPER YABBY** and every state has their own super hero.. (For you DC fans The Batman & The Joker didn't want Superman in Gotham.)
So after a few calls on the **'CAN'** to some of his friends he had the privledge of meeting on his travels around Australia. He managed to get his new-found friend permission to enter the contained, quarantined reminates of the **BIG BRUVA** House, where we were filming the show. Apparently the lower South-West wasn't sunny enough for a nocturnal cooking show?

MAZZ, PANCETTA & TOM-INION PIZZA

INGREDIENTS
1 large pizza base.
100g sliced mozzarella cheese.
2 precooked, diced marron.
3 tbsp créme fraiche.
50g thinly sliced pancetta.
3 tbsp sundried tomatoes.
Small handful of black olives.
Fresh thyme for garnish.

101 WAYS TO COOK MARRON RECIPE SUPPLIED BY
ADAM PURDY
THE TRUE MARRON T.O.T

METHOD
Preheat oven to 220°C and put a baking tray in to heat.
Spread the pizza base with créme fraiche and arrange the mozzarella on top.
Scatter diced marron, pancetta and olives over the pizza base. Sprinkle with a good dose of thyme before baking the pizza for 10-15 minutes or until mozzarella and sauce is bubbling.

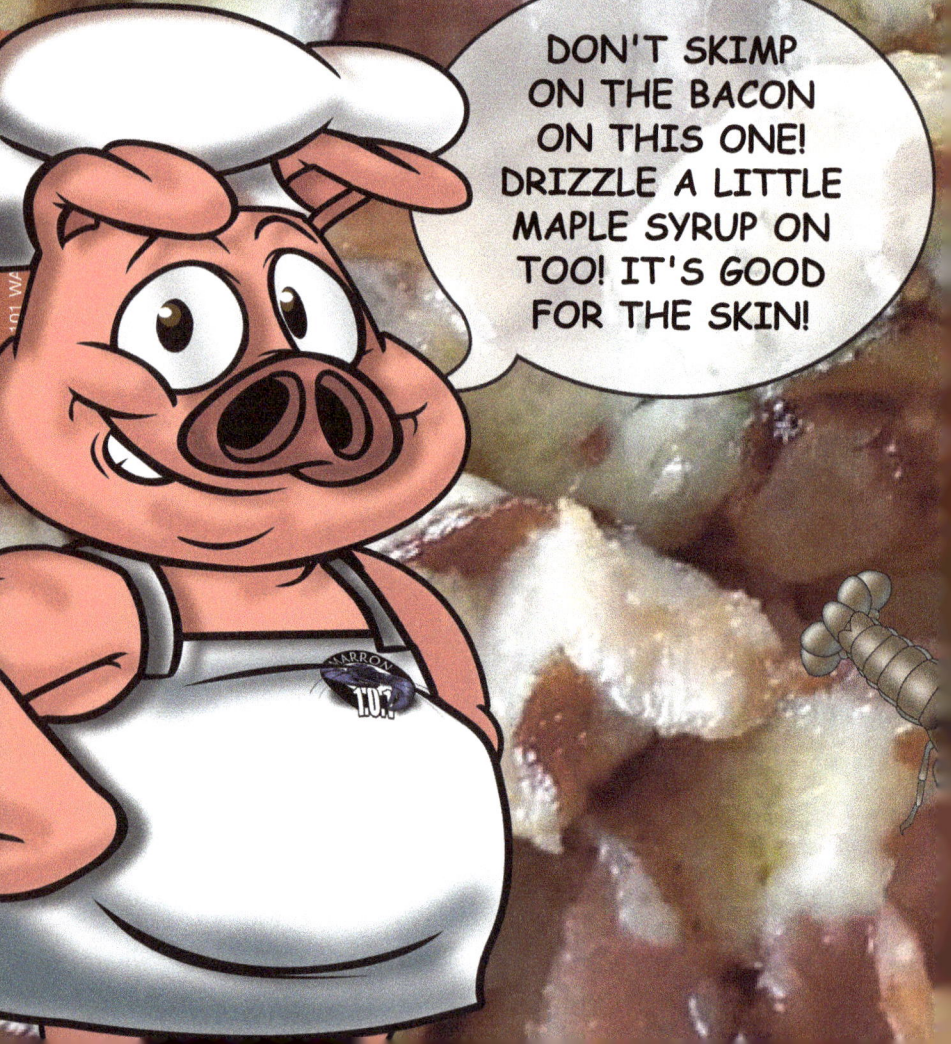

"DON'T SKIMP ON THE BACON ON THIS ONE! DRIZZLE A LITTLE MAPLE SYRUP ON TOO! IT'S GOOD FOR THE SKIN!"

SWEET CHILLI YABBY PIZZA

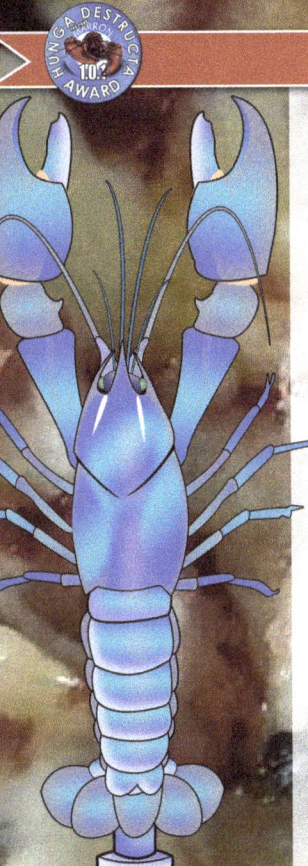

INGREDIENTS
1 x pizza base. (Or make your own).
Tomato paste.
Minced garlic.
Sweet chilli sauce.
Diced bacon.
Spanish onion.
Grated cheese.
2 x cups peeled yabbies.

METHOD
Lightly brush the base with minced garlic and add tomato paste.
Add all other ingredients, leaving the yabbies & cheese until last.
Place yabbies evenly over top of pizza.
and apply sweet chilli sauce.
Add cheese.
I do mine under the griller, as it cooks quicker and the cheese melts better.

PLUS YOU DON'T HAVE TO WAIT SO LONG TO EAT IT!!

YABBIES BELONG IN THE BELLY
Yabbies are an introduced species to WA.
They are native to New South Wales, Victoria and South Australia, and were stocked into farm dams WA in 1932 and after gaining access to the aquifer and underground creeks, yabbies can now be found in and around South-West rivers and dams, keep your eye out for them!

YABBIES CAN BE FISHED ALL YEAR ROUND *HINT *HINT!
Yabbies are much smaller than marron and rarely grow to 130mm in length, making them perfect for Pizzas and Cocktails.

MUSTARD MARRON PIZZA

INGREDIENTS
Marron.
Mustard.
Mayonaise.

PREFFERRED PIZZA TOPPINGS:
Cheese, pineapple, olives, capcicum, mushrooms, honey pepper pumpkin chunks..

METHOD
Mix mayonaise and mustard together,
spread over wrap or pizza.
Add favourite pizza toppings.
Place in oven at 180 °c until cooked.

This chef is on fire! Time to heat things up!

SWEET BERRY MARRON PIZZA

INGREDIENTS
Marron.
Blackberry Jam.
Prefferred pizza toppings.

(NO ANCHOVIES)

METHOD
Mix mayonaise and mustard together, spread over wrap or pizza.
Add favourite pizza toppings.
Place in oven at 180 °c until cooked.

COOK FOR SIX TO SEVEN MINUTES.

101 ways to cook marron recipe supplied by: SHANTEL BERGROTH — THE TRUE MARRON 1.0.1
101 ways to cook marron picture supplied by: SHANTEL BERGROTH — THE TRUE MARRON 1.0.1

RED HOT CHILLI PEPPERS
THE TRUE MARRON
1.0.1

101 WAYS TO COOK MARRON

"WITH OUR 35K SHU'S EACH SHARE, THE BAND SHOULD BE CALLED 'DEEP PURPLE'!"

HALF-TIME ENTERTAINMENT

DAALINY* PEPPERONI & MARRON PIZZA

101 WAYS TO COOK MARRON RECIPE SUPPLIED BY: **BLAZE PEARL** *THE TRUE MARRON 1.0.1*

INGREDIENTS
1 large pizza base.
3 tbsp passata sauce.
1 cup sliced mozzarella cheese.
1 precooked, sliced marron.
2/3 sliced pepperoni.
1 sliced black pearl pepper.
1/2 sliced green pepper.
Fresh mint leaves.
Black pepper.
Sultanas.

METHOD
Preheat oven to 220ºC and put a baking tray in to heat.
Spread the pizza base with passata and arrange the mozzarella on top.
Scatter chunks of marron, pepperoni, sultanas, green & black pearl peppers and sprinkle with ground black pepper.
Bake the pizza for 10-15 minutes or until mozzarella and sauce is bubbling.
Garnish with fresh mint leaves and serve.

*DAALINY IS NOONGAR FOR TONGUE OF FIRE!

GLAMPERS SPICY FLATBREAD

INGREDIENTS
1/2 tsp mustard seeds.
1/2 tsp corriander.
1/2 tsp cumin seeds.
1/2 tsp dried chilli flakes.
3 tbsp olive oil.
1 thinly sliced onion.
1 crushed garlic clove.
2 tbsp coriander leaves, loosely chopped.
3 tomatoes cut into wedges.
2 flatbreads.
2 slice marron (1 per flatbread).
1/2 cup grated cheese.

METHOD
Grind the spices with a blender to a rough powder prior to leaving for camp.
Preheat the flatbread over the fire prior to assembly. Heat the oil in a frying pan and fry the onions and spices until starting to caramelise.
Add the garlic, marron and tomatoes to the pan and cook for a further 3 minutes.
Stir in the coriander leaves then divide the mixture between the two flatbreads and heavily garnish with cheese and sprinkle with black pepper.
Put back over the flames for a further 8 minutes or until the tops are bubbling.

101 WAYS TO COOK MARRON

Every 'OFF' road adventure requires a reliable mechanic!

101 WAYS TO COOK MARRON
BORN 'CRAW'LER CRAY-Z AWARD
PAUL HARFOUCHE
THE TRUE MARRON 1.0.1

MARRON SOUP WITH RISONI

INGREDIENTS
Sam Remo Risoni 500g.
50mls pernot.
400g tomato passata.
3 tomatoes, finely diced.
1 fennel bulb, diced.
1 onion, diced.
2 celery stalk, diced.
1 litre fish stock.
4 marron, whole.
1 lemon, juice and zest.
3mls sunflower oil.
1 bunch of dill, chopped for garnishing.

METHOD
Poach the marron in boiling water for 1 minute. Remove tails from heads and using scissors, cut out the tail meat and reserve. Place marron heads and tail shells into the oven and cook until roasted and the colour has changed to red. Heat the sunflower oil in a saucepan then add half the onion, fennel and celery and fry gently. Add the marron heads and fry for a few minutes, then add the Pernot and cook until reduced by half. Add 1L of fish stock, the tomato passata and a pinch of saffron. Bring to the boil then simmer for 20 minutes. Cook the pasta following the instructions on the packet.
Strain the marron broth through a colander – use a ladle to press the shells down to extract the most flavour possible – then strain again through a fine sieve. Heat the broth to a simmer and add the marron tail meat, cooked risoni, tomatoes and the remaining onion, fennel and celery.
Once the marron is cooked add the chopped dill, lemon juice and zest. Serve garnished with dill sprigs.

MARRON HEAD SOUP

INGREDIENTS
7 fresh caught marron.
Keep the largest marron heads for presentation (if in large shallow bowl).
1 tbsp tomato paste.
2 tsp plain flour.
1-1½ cups of fish stock.
2 tbsp thin cream.
Pinch of cayenne pepper.
2 tbsp olive oil.
3 diced tomatoes.
Juice of ¼ lemon.
20ml cognac.
80ml white wine.
1 finely sliced french shallot.
½ cup finely diced fennel.
2 sprigs of fresh thyme.
2 fresh bay leaf.
1 finely chopped garlic clove.
Salt & freshly ground black pepper.
2 tbsp finely sliced chives.

METHOD
Detach the marron heads from the body and remove the flesh from the tails. Put the heads and shells aside. Thinly slice or dice the raw flesh, then put the tails in the Esky. Heat the olive oil in a large cast-iron pan over the campfire. When very hot, add the marron heads & tail flesh and lightly stir for 3-5 minutes or until the heads change to a nice red (Marron shell will dry instantly when ready, like eggs do) Add the fennel, shallot, thyme and bay leaves.
Give it a good stir before adding the tomato paste then add the diced tomatoes and flour.
Combine the cognac, wine & stock in a jar before adding to the pan. Reduce the heat to medium-low and simmer for 20 minutes.
Stir in the thin cream, cayenne pepper & lemon juice and cook for a further 5 minutes.
Strain the marron sauce through a strainer into a saucepan. Firmly but gently (as not to crack them) squeeze the marron heads to extract as much flavour as possible.
To serve, gently reheat the marron tails in the broth and season to taste with salt, pepper & garlic to taste.

101 WAYS TO COOK MARRON RECIPE SUPPLIED BY
RHIANNON COOMBS
THE TRUE MARRON 1.0.1

ADVICE FROM THE BIG BLACK BOOT

Besides having a nice feed of crayfish on the banks of a creek, there is no better source of protein than our good ol' freshwater mussels. Finding them in the wild come from a little skill and understanding of our river systems. So grab your **BIG BLACK BOOTS** and head to your nearest substantial freshwater creek and lets see what we can find! Mussells can breed all year round, but their main spawning period is spring & summer. So if you are out and **'A BOOT'** in this period, please be mindful to not go overboard and keep an eye out babies. Now you are out at your local creek or riverway, it is essential for you to check the water quality before beginning your search. Areas with heavy boat activity or close to farms and towns, may have pollutants that could make you quite sick. We also advise for you to stay away from stagnant water pools above the high tide line. The best time to go foraging for mussels is at low tide. This makes the larger mussels more accessible. Grab a tide chart for your local area for accurate timing. Mussels are normally found in the soft sediment sands in free flowing creeks. This allows them to siphon filter food as the current passes. Once you have found your location, it's time to make sure you pick only the ones good for eating. First off, the bigger the better! The larger mussels are normally more tender than the smaller ones & it gives the smaller ones a chance at reproducing. Only grab mussels that are closed, if they are open they are probably dead and should not be eaten. Cleaning mussels can be quite time consuming depending on if they have barnacles attached or a fine layer of algae, either way you want to make sure you remove anything that can ruin the taste. Most mussel species have '**HAIRY BEARDS**', you definately want to remove this prior to cooking. To remove it, simply grab it between your fingers and pull it toward the joining of the shells. It should come off quite easy, but if you have any problems just scrape it off with a knife. The good thing is we don't have to sit around drooling over mussels while they take time to purge. Mussels feed by filtering, so soaking them in clean water for 15 minutes (longer may kill the mussels) should be enough to remove any sediments from the inside of the shell. All the sediment will be left at the bottom of the container. Lift the mussels out of the water gently, this will prevent them from absorbing anymore of the discarded sediment. If any of them have opened, give them a light tap on the shell. If the close they are still alive, if not, best to discard it.

TREAD LIGHTLY OUT THERE!

My Boy Eli!

> HI I'M ELI!, THANK YOU FOR BUYING DADS BOOK! SEE YOU ALL SOON!

CRAY-Z IS AS CRAY-Z DOES — THE TRUE MARRON 1.0.1

101 WAYS TO COOK MARRON

Adam G Purdy

COBBA WITH WEDGES

101 WAYS TO COOK MARRON PICTURE SUPPLIED BY: TANDANUS 'COBBA' BOSKOCKI — THE TRUE MARRON 1.0.1

101 WAYS TO COOK MARRON PICTURE SUPPLIED BY: KEVIN KNIGHT — THE TRUE MARRON 1.0.1

INGREDIENTS
500g wedges.
1 onion, finely chopped.
1 clove garlic, crushed.
1 tbsp balsamic vinegar.
2 x 400g tinned cherry tomatoes.
1 tsp white caster sugar.
500g skinned & boned cobbler fillets.
1/2 tbsp olive oil.
100g kale for garnish.

METHOD
Preheat the oven to 200°C, fan 180°C, gas 6. Put the wedges on a large baking tray in a single layer and cook for 20 minutes. Meanwhile, put the onion, garlic, vinegar, tomatoes and sugar in a pan and bring to the boil.
Turn the heat down to low and simmer for 10 minutes, stirring frequently.
Line a baking tray with foil. Brush the fish fillets with the oil, season with plenty of freshly ground black pepper and arrange on the tray.
Put in the oven with the wedges for the final 10 minutes of cooking time.
Put the kale in a microwave-proof bowl with 2 tablespoons water, cover loosely with cling film and cook on high for 1 minute & 30 seconds. Serve with the fish, wedges and cherry tomato sauce.

DON'T FORGET YOUR SIDE OF MARRON WITH THIS ONE!

CAMPFIRE PAN-FRIED COBBA & MAZZ

101 WAYS TO COOK MARRON PICTURE SUPPLIED BY TANDANUS 'COBBA' BOSKOCKI THE TRUE MARRON T.O.T

INGREDIENTS
4 river cobbler fillets.
2 tbsp olive oil.
1 onion, finely chopped.
2 garlic cloves, finely chopped.
1 green chilli, remove seeds & finely chopped.
1 tsp mustard seeds.
1 tsp cumin seeds.
2 tsp garam masala.
200g red lentils.
400g tin chopped tomatoes.
600ml low salt vegestock.
240g pack of baby spinach.
handful fresh coriander, chopped, plus a few extra sprigs to serve.

NAAN TO SERVE.

METHOD
Heat 1 tbsp of the oil in a pan. Cook the onion for 5 minutes, then stir in the garlic and chilli and cook for 1 minute more.
Add the mustard and cumin seeds and 1 tsp garam masala; cook for a further 2 minutes.
Stir in the lentils, tomatoes and stock and bring to the boil. Reduce the heat and simmer, covered, for 20 minutes. Meanwhile, rub the remaining oil and garam masala over the fillets. Heat a large pan and fry the fish, over lowmedium heat, for 3-4 minutes each side, or until cooked through.
Stir the spinach and coriander through the lentils, until just starting to wilt. Season well.
Divide the lentil mixture between 4 plates and top each with a piece of fish. Garnish with a few coriander sprigs and serve with naan on the side, if you like.

DRY MARRON COOKUP

101 WAYS TO COOK MARRON RECIPE SUPPLIED BY LIMETTA CITRON THE TRUE MARRON T.O.T

INGREDIENTS
2kg shells still on the marron.
Extra virgin olive oil.
Lemon juice.
Ginger.
Garlic.
Coriander.
Shallot.
Green Peppy.
Salt.
Pepper.
Ultimate DJAM Shredder Waste.
0.25 cup water.

METHOD
Pound together coriander, chillies, ginger, garlic, olive oil & lemon juice in a mortar. pestle to a rough paste and set aside.
Add oil to a hot wok pan.
Salt Mazz pieces with shells still on & add to wok, adding more oil as necessary - do not allow to stick or burn. Cook for six to seven minutes. Add a little water to steam him. Mix through curry paste.
Just before removing from heat, add chop-ped shallot stalk, juice of one lemon, season with pepper & **DJAM S.W.** Hide the evidence on a large plate or platter and top with coriander leaves and shallots.

HELP GET OUR NATURAL HABITATS BACK!

GO TO THE BACK OF THE BOOK TO SEE HOW YOU CAN HELP!

GARLIC GIVES YOU MARRON MUSSELS

INGREDIENTS
1 kg fresh mussels.
4 marron tails, precooked & minced.
3 cloves garlic, minced.
3 tbsp butter.
1 cup heavy cream.
1/2 cup dry white wine.
Salt to taste.

METHOD
Preheat the campfire for cooking.
In a small to medium foil pan, heat butter and garlic over the fire until garlic is slightly golden. You will have to act fast as it will cook quickly.
Add cream and simmer for a couple minutes before removing from the fire.
Add the wine, marron and mussels and gently turn to coat. Cover with foil and return to the fire to cook for approximately 5-7 minutes or until the shells have opened. Shake occasionally but gently to coat with the sauce while it cooks. Discard any unopened mussels. Season with salt to taste and serve hot.

SMOTHERED IN CREAMY GARLIC SAUCE.

DRUNKEN MAZZ & GINGERED MUSSELS

INGREDIENTS
1 large pan of cleaned and soaked mussels.
4 marron tails, finely diced.
2 tbs garlic oil.
Juice of half a lemon.
Thumb of ginger – finely diced.
½ can of ale (or more if you like it strong!).
½ cup of water (adjust this to the size of your pan).
Large handful of roughly chopped spinach or dandelion leaves.

METHOD
Heat the oil in a large pan then add the ginger. Cook until starting to brown. Add the mussels, marron, water and beer to the pan, turn up the heat and cover the pan with a lid. Once the pan starts to steam, continue to cook for another 3-4 minutes, shaking the pan every now and then. The marron will cook quickly, your indication on when they will be ready is when the mussels have opened up to be served. If any of the mussels are still closed after cooking then they should be discarded unless they can be opened easily.
Squeeze the lemon juice over the mussels & marron.

SERVE WITH A HUNK OF WELL-BUTTERED CRUSTY BREAD.

ALUNIOS CREEK FOOD BASKET

INGREDIENTS
2kg freshwater mussels.
2 fillets of cobbler, skinned & boned.
10 cloves garlic roughly chopped.
6 chopped marron.
1 red onion, diced.
2 chopped leek stalks.
Cleaned & prepared into inch long sections of common reed root.
3 tbsp pesto sauce (suit your taste).
3 beers of your choice.
2 tbsp butter.

METHOD
First things first, make sure your heat source is nice and hot! If you are cooking over a campfire, ensure that your coals are red hot and throwing off some really nice heat. Add in the butter and allow to melt. Once butter is melted toss in leeks, onions, garlic, common reed root and allow them to soften and brown slightly.
Mix in the pesto.
Meanwhile heat up some oil in another pan and toss in the cobbler fillets and the inch long sections of common reed. Fry these like chips, until golden and have a crisp crunch.
Add the mussels & marron into the pot and using your hands or large spoon, toss to ensure everything is coated in the pesto mixture.
Now time to crack a beer.
One beer is added, place top on pot and allow the mussels & marron to steam and cook.
Check in every 3-5 minutes and give everything a good stir, bringing what is on bottom to the top.
Let mussels & marron cook for 8-10 minutes. Once mussels look completed, (should of opened) remove from heat and serve immediately in pot with fresh common reed damper and common reed root fried chips.

TASTES LIKE POTATO.

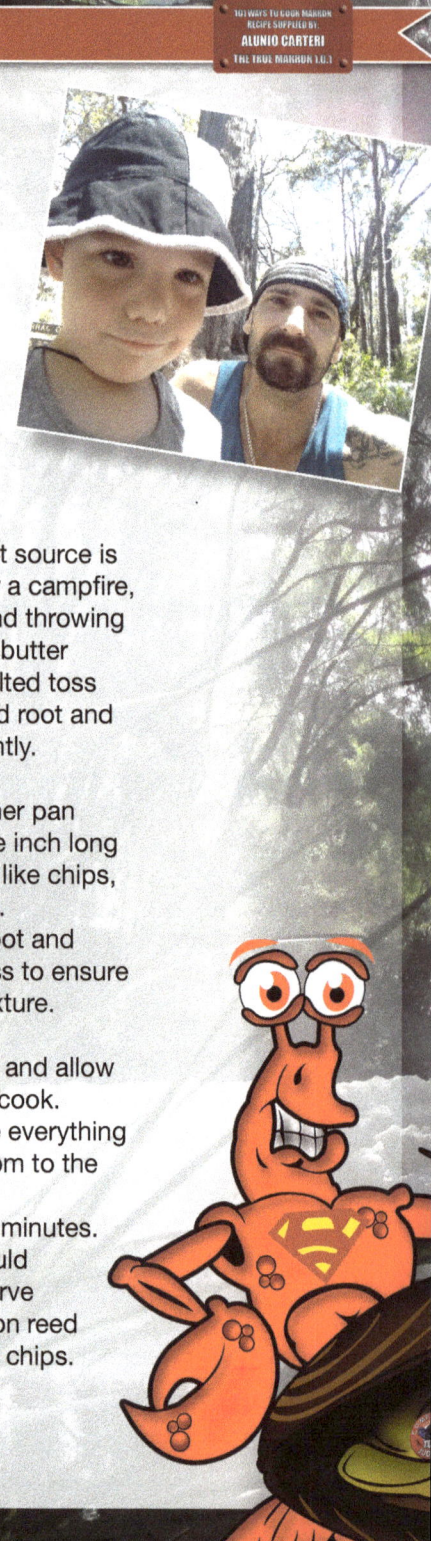

MARRON & TOMATO RISOTTO

INGREDIENTS
150g pre-cooked, peeled marron tail.
2 cups of tomato passata.
2 tbsp olive oil.
3 cloves of crushed garlic.
2 tbsp créme fraiche.
Small handful of shredded coriander leaves.
1 finely chopped onion.
1/3 cup risotto rice.
2 cups of fish stock.

METHOD
Put the fish stock and passata in a saucepan and put it on a medium heat.
Heat the oil in a smaller pan and lightly fry the onions, enough for the oil to activate the onion but not colour it.
Add your garlic (the more the merrier, I say!). Cook for a further 2 minutes before stirring in the rice. Once the rice, onion & garlic are covered in oil, add 1/3 of the heated fish stock.
Stir occasionally until magority of the stock has been absorbed into the rice.
Add another 1/3 of the stock every 15 minutes until the rice is nice and squishy, but bouncy.. You don't want the rice to go to mush.
Thinly slice then add the marron and créme fraiche and give it a good stir before taking off of the heat and let sit for 5 mintues to heat through the marron flesh.
Before serving, season with salt & pepper and the shredded coriander.

MARRON SOUP

INGREDIENTS
Shredded marron.
Lemon juice.
1 Large cup of boiling water.
Roasted veges.
2 tbs chicken stock powder.
Garlic powder.
1 tbs chilli.
1 tbs tomato paste.
Worcestershire sauce.
Finely chopped celery.

METHOD
Put roast veges in the blender, add 1 large cup of boiling water mixed with 2 tablespoons of chicken stock, garlic powder, chilli, tomato paste and a squirt of worcestershire sauce.
Add shredded marron and 1 finely chopped celery.
Blend and serve hot or cold.

CRISPY MARRON

INGREDIENTS
500g raw marron.
2 tsp light soy.
1 tbsp Chinese rice wine or dry sherry.
1 tsp five spice powder.
1/4 tsp freshly ground black pepper.
450ml ground nut oil.
8 tbsp cornflour.
2 eggs, beaten.
10 tbsp breadcrumbs.

METHOD
Peel marron, discarding shells.
Using a small sharp knife partially split the marron lengthways.
Pat the marron dry with kitchen paper.
Mix the marron with the soy sauce, rice wine, five spice powder and pepper.
Heat wok and add oil.
While the oil is heating dip the marron in the cornflour, shaking gently to remove any excess.
Dip into the beaten egg and coat thoroughly with breadcrumbs.
When the oil begins to smoke lightly deep fry the coated marron until golden.
Drain well on kitchen paper.

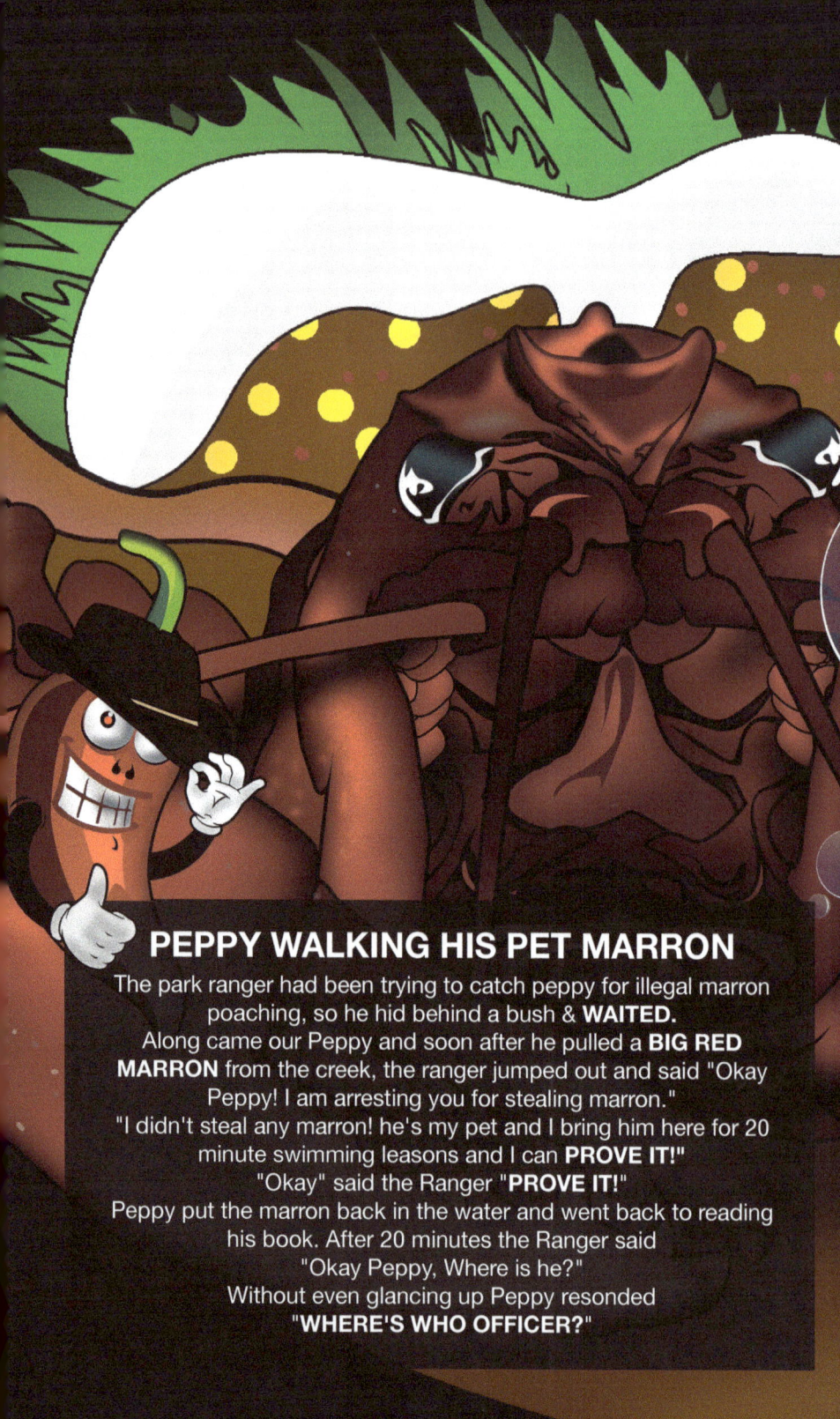

PEPPY WALKING HIS PET MARRON

The park ranger had been trying to catch peppy for illegal marron poaching, so he hid behind a bush & **WAITED**.
Along came our Peppy and soon after he pulled a **BIG RED MARRON** from the creek, the ranger jumped out and said "Okay Peppy! I am arresting you for stealing marron."
"I didn't steal any marron! he's my pet and I bring him here for 20 minute swimming leasons and I can **PROVE IT!**"
"Okay" said the Ranger "**PROVE IT!**"
Peppy put the marron back in the water and went back to reading his book. After 20 minutes the Ranger said
"Okay Peppy, Where is he?"
Without even glancing up Peppy resonded
"WHERE'S WHO OFFICER?"

THE UNDROPPABLE FALAFEL

INGREDIENTS

FALAFELS
300g minced marron tail.
A can chickpeas, drained.
4 cloves garlic, roughly chopped.
1 shallot, roughly chopped.
2 tbsp freshly chopped parsley.
1 tsp ground cumin.
1 tsp ground coriander.
3 tbsp all-purpose flour.
MACON salt.
Freshly ground black pepper.
Vegetable oil, for frying.

YOGURT SAUCE
1/2 cup Greek yogurt.
Juice of 1 lemon.
1 tbsp extra-virgin olive oil.
1 tbsp freshly chopped dill.
Pinch of salt.
Freshly ground black pepper.

TAHINI SAUCE
1/2 cup tahini.
1 garlic clove, minced.
1 tbsp lemon juice.
2 tbsp warm water
(more as needed).
Lemon salt or shaved lemon.

SERVING
Pitas (Pita Bread).
Select your favourite
simple salad fillings.

METHOD

FALAFELS
Combine chickpeas, garlic, shallot, parsley, cumin, coriander, flour and season with salt & pepper.
blend in a food processor, don't over do it though!
Add your minced marron tail, mix together with the herbal blend until combined.
Mould your falafels into 'meatball' size balls, squeeze to compact.
Put them in the refrigerator to chill while you preheat your pan.
Fry falafels until golden.
Transfer to a paper towel-lined plate and season immediately with **MACON** salt.

YOGURT SAUCE
In a medium bowl, whisk together yogurt, lemon juice, oil, and dill.
(not our little '**DIL**' friend)
Season with salt and pepper.

TAHINI SAUCE
In a medium bowl, whisk together tahini, garlic, lemon juice, and warm water.
Season with lemon salt or shaved lemon.
Serve falafels in pita bread with your simple salad fillings and smother with the sauces.

WHAT HAPPENS WHEN YOU SIT ON A GRAPE?

IT GIVES A LITTLE WINE!

WHERE IS OUR HEAD JUDGE?

Do you think you know what happened to our Head Judge Mazz C. Cainii?
The answer is spread through the titles, ingredients and cooking methods.
The competitors comments and comics scenes are obviously crutial to the case too.
If you think you have found the answers in the pages go to; http://thetruemarron101.au
With 1000 scenerios, but only one winning solution. We can't wait to see what answers you, your friends and family come up with.
The person or family with the correct line up of recipe names and comic references explaining what had happened to our mate Mazz will win the:

'SHELL'OCK HOLMES MERCHANDISE PACK!

WHICH INCLUDES 'THE FINAL SCENE' COMIC ON A RANGE OF OUR MERCHANDISE WITH YOUR AWARDED BADGE OF HONOUR:
1 x A3 Signed Gloss Poster,
1 x Marron 1.0.1 Bar Mat
1 x Marron 1.0.1 T-shirt
FULL SET OF BADGES to match the winning scenerio

EACH SUBMISSION FORM THAT COMES CLOSE TO THE WINNING CORRECT C.I.S.T. FORM RECEIVE:

A 'SHELL'OCK IS ON THE CASE!
Decal for the car, fridge or can be placed in the inside front of back covers of this book.

GOOD LUCK EVERYONE! DAD HAS MADE THIS REALLY HARD! IT'S NOT WHO YOU 'AXE'PECT!

ARE YOU OUR 'SHELL'OCK?

Do you think you have figured out the events that lead to the disappearance of our Head Judge Mazz?
Feel like testing your detective skills?
THEN THE S.W.P.D. NEED YOU!
Get your friends and family involved and see who can come up with the correct recipe names, ingredients, character comments, and comic scenes that explains what happened to our old friend. A quick heads up, the clues arent in page order. You and your team of slueths will have to flick back and forth throughout the pages to create your story. This is a great way to spend an evening around the campfire or while you are locked in your tent while it buckets down outside. The storyline has been set up with clues dropped randomly. We wish you luck and can't wait to see what scenerios come through*.
We have included a few sheets for you to fill out. You can also print the sheets from: thetruemarron101 website
Do not hesitate to submit more than one entry if you want to. The more you enter the more chances of winning.
Once you have completed the Crime Investigation Sleuth Theory (C.I.S.T) document upload it to the thetruemarron101.au website and Sergeant Eli - Head Detective of South-West P.D. will access your submission and let you know your results.

We wish you all luck on your submissions.

Adam T Purdy   Eli Graeme Kanny-Purdy

*All submissions must be on the South West P.D's 'C.I.S.T' form found on the back of the book.
If you are not able to upload the page to the website, please post it to:
P.O. BOX 1045 Manjimup, Western Australia 6258.
or email; adam@thetruemarron101.au
Your theory can only be based on evidence provided throughout the book.
Page numbers you have referenced must be documented for the submission to be accepted.

BUSH BREAD VS DAMPER

The People of the Land were very versitile when it came to their food. The dough/ mcrindjook, mcrinyook (noongar translation) they would make from some of the grains, legumes, roots, nuts & native plants. Bush Bread or Seedcakes as they are called, have struggled to hold any originality since the European settlers came in and adapted the native recipe with western products (pre-milled flour, salt, butter) today referred to as johnny cakes, or a large loaf, known today as damper.

Some of the plants used are; kangaroo grass, pigwig, mulga, prickly wattle, dead finish seed, bush bean and the common reed. The seeds would be crushed into the dough, eaten raw, rolled into bite size pieces or baked in the coals of a fire. The bread/ mariny (noongar translation) is high in protein and carbohydrate, and forms part of a balanced traditional diet. After the grain was collected, it needed to have the chaff removed which was done using the coolamon (dish traditionally used by the People of the Land to carry water or food). It was a multi-purpose carrying vessel. Once all the chaff had been removed, it was ground into a fine powder (flour) this technique has been used for over 50,000 years. If it's not broke, don't fix it!

The flour was mixed with enough water to make a dough that was foldable and wouldn't stick to the fingers while kneading.

This was then chucked directly on the coals, giving the bread a nice crunchy crust. A good way to tell if it is ready is if you can poke a stick into it and it comes out clean.

Now you have the perfect bread time to catch the perfect freshwater feed.

NATIVE SEASONAL SMÖRGÅSBOARD

For people of the land the bush can be a smörgåsboard. By knowing your area and the native plants we have at our fingertips and their benefits, we can save a lot of room when it comes to loading the entire pantry into the back of the car, to spend two nights in the outdoors. For our local Noongar tribes that populated the lower South-West for over 47,000 years prior to english settlement, finding something to nibble on wasn't that hard. They enjoyed a wide range of berries and plants for eating and a feed of kangaroo, emu, birds, turtles, goannas, bardi grubs, marron, swamp crays, fish, mussels, cobbler, abalone and eel was only a good game of hide and seek away.

Adam T Purdy

GET TO KNOW YOUR BUSH TUCKER

I would highly recommend getting the family involved and taking a bushtucker tour of your local region. The more you have available at your fingertips, the more extravagant and flavoursome the meals you can make while camping will get. (and you can save more esky room for the more important things, whatever that may be for you). All people of the land respect nature and what it gives us to help us to survive. The key is to only take what we need to help maintain biodiversity. The more we adapt to the seasons, we can be sure not to deplete the natural resources so they will still be available for the next year.

NOONGAR WORDS TO PRACTICE

DJOOMBAR	**HAIRY**
MARRON	**FRESHWATER CRAYFISH**
Kep midjal	Rain Water
Djilki (Dil)	Swamp Crayfish
Bardi	Witchetty Grub
Yongka	Kangaroo
Weitj	Emu
Nyingarn	Echidna
Ngwir	Possum
Djidong	Small Lizard
Kalbiri	Wild Berries
Nyola	Cobbler
Djirp	Dandelions
Djildjit	Fish
Koorni	Frog
Mereny	Food
Kardar	Racehorse Goanna
Dilert	Blue Tongue Lizard
Booyi	Long Neck Turtle
Karla	Campfire
Mariny	Bread
Dartj/Daadja	Meat

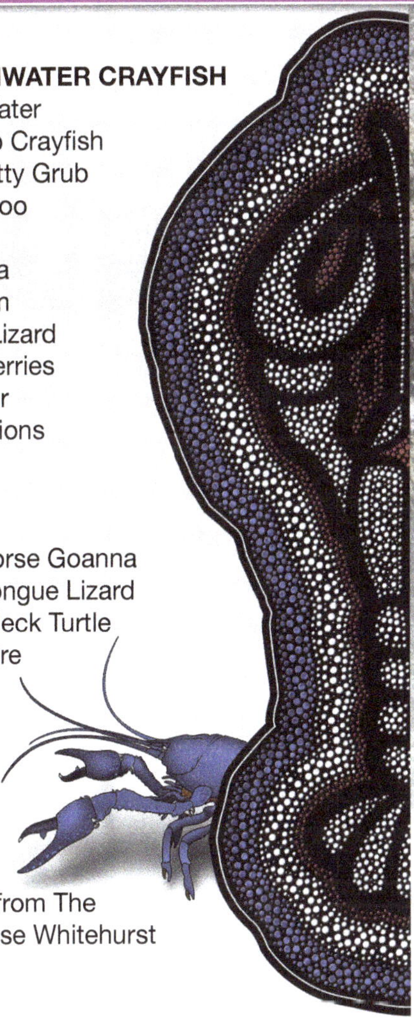

These and other translations came from The Noongar Dictonary Compiled by Rose Whitehurst First Edition 1992.

TRADITIONAL NOONGAR SEASONS

The people of the land have traditionally adapted their food gathering and hunted acording to their six seasons. By translation, the season names told them what resources are the most plentiful for that duration of time.

BIRAK (DECEMBER - JANUARY)

Represented by the colour red for sun, fire & heat. Birak is the season for fires, with the Easterly winds in the morning & evening winds from the South-West, the Noongar people would use fires to burn all the lower shrubbery. This would help a lot of the hardy bush plants germinate and make it easier for crossing the land. Animals would also benefit (once all the screaming and burning is done) from the fresh new shoots that pop out of the ashes. With water levels decreasing through this season, it's a good time to get to those deeper parts of the waterholes to find the larger marron. The Tadpoles have grown their legs and are leaving the puddles, Snakes shed their skins and lay on the rocks absorbing the heat. Some baby birds are taking the brave leap out of their nests, while others are squawking at their parents feet for a regurgitated feed.

BUNURU (FEBRUARY - MARCH)

Bunuru is represented by the colour orange and with little to no rain and hot easterly winds making inland humid and muggy. Bunuru is the hottest time of year making it the perfect time to be spending the days by the waterholes, creeks or down the coast. Fresh water and salt water fish, crayfish, abalone being served with watercress, river-side reeds, seaweed, plants & flowers. Bees are in full swing collecting from our forest giants; jarrah, karri, marri & gum trees are all blooming.

DJERAN (APRIL - MAY)

Green is the perfect colour to represent Djeran, the beginning of cooler weather brings in new shoots of grass and everything that had turned orange now turns green. Moisture in the air leaves the morning with a thick fog, barely penetrable with even todays strongest LED lights. Flying ants are in an abundance, and frogs have found their voices (probably what makes them so easy to catch this time of year). Djeran would of been the period to prepare for the cold winter coming. Homes and shelters would of been updated and repaired and seeds and grains being stored Some would move inland or to higher grounds and re-establish a camp.

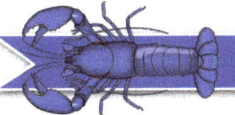

MAKURU (JUNE - JULY)

Makuru brings in the coldest part of the year for the South-West, so dark-blue seems to be a fitting colour for this season. Endless days of freezing rains and bone-chilling fronts bring in the kangaroo and heartier meals. They are are a necessity to warm the hearts and souls of your tribe members. Bush stews and roasts, bringing people together before finding a partner to snuggle with to beat the sudden drops in temperture as the dusk draws near. Many animals will partner up in this time of year in preparation for the up-and-coming mating season; birds, wombats, kangaroos. Many other native animals will use their body heat to sedjuce the opposite sex. This is the season to present your partner with a new fur coat (bwoka).

DJILBA (AUGUST - SEPTEMBER)

What do you think of when you see pink? Hopefully you think of flowers. Djilba all of the wildflowers and plants are in full bloom in the South-West. Land based animals are main on the menu including possum (ngwir) and emu (waitj) The male (kelang) and female (koomool) possums, teaching their young how to forage for food. The magpie (Koolbardi) is in full attack mode protecting their 'Boomeranger' nestlings. It's the season of growth. The kangaroo mob is getting larger, as the Buck (Male Roo) teaches the others in the court how to box. Dordok (pigs) teach the piglets how to dig for wild truffle. As the moons pass and the tempretures rise, the grass trees flower rise with it as the season draws to an end.

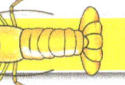

KAMBARANG (OCTOBER - NOVEMBER)

With the turning of the season the symbolic colour for Kambarang is yellow, this makes sense when you see the abundance of yellow flowers throughout the South-West come to life in this period of time. From our very own Christmas tree with its orange and bright yellow flowers. The kangaroo paw and acacias are popping their heads out above the foliage. Our reptile friends are coming out of hibernation and are seeking out the warm spots to gather their energy for a long awaited meal. All are indications of the warmer weather around the corner.

MEET OUR CRAY-Z COMPANIES

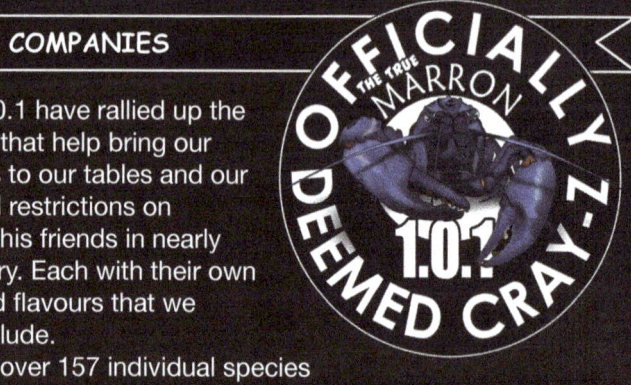

The True Marron 1.0.1 have rallied up the Cray-Z Companies that help bring our favourite Mud-bugs to our tables and our lives. With seasonal restrictions on catching Mazz and his friends in nearly every state & country. Each with their own unique varieties and flavours that we cannot forget to include.

Australia alone has over 157 individual species of freshwater crayfish, many who are protected for good reason due to over fishing and territorial fights with invading species.

So supporting the Cray-Z Companies and purchasing our Crays & friends through them helps protect our waterways from over fishing and will allow our 10-legged friends to thrive in their natural habitats, wherever that may be. Our Offically Deemed Cray-Z Companies have dedicated their lives to making crayfish & their friends available for purchase to the general public.

GO TO: THETRUEMARRON101.AU/CRAY-Z-COMPANIES
EVEN A RANGE OF RESTAURANTS AROUND AUSTRALIA AND & THE WORLD WHO TAKE ALL THE HARD WORK OUT OF IT.
NOW YOU CAN ENJOY YOUR FAVOURITE MEAL
WITHOUT THE DISHES TOO!

BECOME A LEGEND WITH A LEGEND IN A LEGEND

SPEND $200 WITH ANY OF OUR SPONSORS.
TAKE A PHOTO OF YOUR RECEIPT &
EMAIL IT TO: ADAM@THETRUEMARRON101.AU
YOU WILL RECIEVE A:

KARKINOS ASTACUS II
DECAL OR POSTER (YOUR CHOICE) FOR YOUR CAR OR HOME,
WITH YOUR VERY OWN
GOT'CHA KANKLE AWARD.
THIS WILL BE SHOWCASED IN THETRUEMARRON101.AU
WEBSITE'S WINNERS & PARTICIPANTS SECTION.
JUST OUR WAY OF SAYING "THANK YOU"
FOR SUPPORTING THESE CRAY-Z COMPANIES,
PUTTING OUR FAVOURITE BUGS ON OUR TABLE.

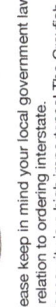

Please keep in mind your local government laws & restrictions in relation to ordering interstate.
Biosecurity is a high importance! The Crayfish may not see the line we have marked on the ground, but YOU CAN! Legal penalties can apply if state restrictions are broken. Please respect all of our amazing companies helping us keep our mud-bugs "ALIVE & CLICKING for the AUSTRALIAN PUBLIC!"

GENERAL PUBLIC SUPPLIERS

 1. FOREST FRESH MARRON - W.A.
FORESTFRESHMARRON.COM.AU

 2. OLD VASSE TROUT & MARRON FARM - W.A.
OLDVASSETROUTANDMARRONFARM.COM.AU

 3. KANGAROO ISLAND MARRON FARM - S.A.
KANGAROOISLANDMARRON.COM

PETS & PROS

 4. YABBY DABBA DOO - N.S.W.
YABBYDABBADOO.AU

 5. PLACES AQUA - W.A.
PASESAQUA.COM.AU

 6. MERV COOPERS CRAZY CRABS - W.A.
CRAZYCRABS.COM.AU

7. WOODVALE FISH AND LILY FARM - W.A.
CRAZYCRABS.COM.AU

CRAY-Z SUBJECTS

 MARRON GROWERS ASSOCIATION - W.A.
MARRONGROWERS.ORG

 MARGARET RIVER CONSERVATION CENTRE - W.A.
NATURECONSERVATION.ORG.AU

 EAST MANJIMUP PRIMARY SCHOOL - W.A.
NATURECONSERVATION.ORG.AU

101 WAYS TO COOK MARRON
GOT CHA KANKLE AWARD
KARKINOS ASTACUS II
THETRUEMARRON 1.0.1

FOREST FRESH MARRON - W.A.

FOREST FRESH MARRON PEMBERTON

SEASONAL OPENING HOURS CALL AHEAD OR CHECK THE SIGNS OUT THE FRONT

SUCCULENT SOUTH-WEST MARRON
(FRESHWATER LOBSTER)

DELIVERY TO ALL MAJOR & MANY SECONDARY AIRPORTS COUNTRY WIDE.

All Marron sold through Forest Fresh Marron are farmed sustainably in either ponds or dams which mimic the natural environment. This type of farming has an extremely low impact on the environment and provides a chemical and antibiotic "free range" for the marron to develop.

Come in for a visit to take some marron home for dinner! At the same time, you can give the kids a thrill at seeing the live animals. we would prefer for you to cook your own succulent marron feast as this a large part of the experience but, if you have time to wait, we can cook your marron for you for a small fee.

Transport packs available to keep your marron alive for up to 24+ hours.

We can send live marron to most places, please call us to place your order.

BUS TOUR GROUPS STOPS BY APPOINTMENT ONLY

Call +61 436 487 188
forestfreshmarron@outlook.com
LOT 5 PUMP HILL RD
PEMBERTON WA 6258

CRAY-Z COMPANIES

ORDERING MARRON FROM FOREST FRESH

WE CAN ASSIST WITH SUPPLYING JUVENILLES FOR DAM STOCK.

As marron are a seasonal produce, availability changes daily so please call to see how we can help you. Packaging and freight costs are additional and depend on weight and location.

WE ARE HAPPY TO HELP YOU OVER THE PHONE.

+61 436 487 188

When you order from Forest Fresh Marron you are buying direct from the farm. Forest Fresh Marron is supplied by over 60 local marron growers. By sourcing our marron from local producers, we can maintain a consistent, reliable, high quality product throughout the year.

Our facility holds Marron for a limited time enabling distribution from a single point. Within 24 hours of being ordered your live marron will be delivered to your doorstep (within Perth area) or to all major and many secondary airports country wide. We prefer to talk one on one, marron are sent live so it is important to get the delivery details correct to protect their freshness. If you would prefer to place your order online:

FORESTFRESHMARRON.COM.AU

USE: TTMARRON101 AS A REFERENCE WHEN ORDERING ONLINE

OLD VASSE TROUT & MARRON FARM - W.A.

LOCATED ON THE CORNER OF:
OLD VASSE ROAD & PEMBERTON-NORTHCLIFFE ROAD
PEMBERTON, WESTERN AUSTRALIA 6258

BOOK YOUR GROUP TODAY! (+618) 9776 1726
OLDVASSETROUTANDMARRONFARM.COM.AU

WHAT THEIR VISITOR HAVE TO SAY

IAN KIDD OCTOBER 2020
Great place to enjoy a few hours with the family and a very good chance of catching a feed.
The trout I caught (700 g) tasted fantastic. The staff were very friendly and helpful. Highly recommended

ED JUDY FALLENS JULY 2019
Awesome Awesome Awesome
Love fishing Love Trout

TONY MAGON JANUARY 2018
Certainly plenty of fish in there had a good morning and my son caught his first fish and than another 4 And plenty of other bites too.

JESS RAY WHITE OCTOBER 2017
Had a fantastic afternoon at Old Vasse Trout & Marron Farm with my husband & 2 young kids. Well setup with lovely grass area for the kids, had a great time and caught trout within 10 minutes from being there. will definitely came again!
Thanks Justin!

Barry Rushton February 2018
Went with my grandson,caught some BIG fish,said it was one of the best days of his life, happy days.

101 WAYS TO COOK MARRON
GOT US HOOKED AWARD
OLD VASSE TROUT & MARRON
THE TRUE MARRON 1.0.1

KANGAROO ISLAND MARRON FARM - S.A.

Kangaroo Island Marron Farm is a family owned business that is dedicated to bringing you the ethically farm grown Marron.

We purge our marron for 48 hours. Purging is the process where stock is held and fed. This allows them to empty their digestive system prior to sale.

Marron are then put into hibernation in a cool room by chilling the water at 11 °C, this maintains the marron in perfect condition for live transportation.

YOU SIMPLY CAN'T GET ANY FRESHER THAN LIVE!

OUR CRAYFISH ARE AVAILABLE IN A NUMBER OF SIZES

YABBIES	SML MARRON	MED MARRON	LGE MARRON
MIXED SIZES	6-8 PER KG	4-5 PER KG	2-3 PER KG

You can pick them up directly from our farm. Please make sure to call ahead so that we can ensure we have a sufficient number already purged for you to pick up & take away that way you can enjoy them at their highest quality.

PLEASE EMAIL JUSTIN & JULIE
GOLDBERG@SENET.COM.AU OR CALL 0427 797 298
KANGAROOISLANDMARRON.COM

THE FAMILY BEHIND THE BUSINESS

Family member Justin Le Cornu is a qualified chef. After many years in the industry working as a commercial chef, one day he saw on television a program on Kangaroo Island Marron. Impressed with the Marron and their suitability to commercial restaurants (as they were able to be kept alive in a dormant state in the fridge for a number of days) made them a very attractive addition to any menu.
This interest in the species lef Justin to commence an investigation as to how to regularly source them. At the time there was no constant supply of them, so he decided he would investigate the growning of them. During the process he found the he liked the lifestyle and decided that he would move to Kangaroo Island with his wife and became dedicated to growing Marron.

We are situated centrally in the island, just west outside of Parndana along the Playford Highway (4327 Playfor Hwy), approximately a half an hour drive from Kingscote.

YABBY DABBA DOO - N.S.W.

SCHOOL GROUPS ARE FREE!

MUMS, DADS, GRANDIES & THE KIDS BORED DURING THE HOLIDAYS? COMPLAINING OF NOTHING TO DO?

COME YABBYING THE OLD FASHIONED WAY WITH A PIECE OF MEAT ON A STRING!

(More fun than Netflix, Stan, Snapchat, I-Pads, Xboxes or Playstations! Just ask your Pop!)

YABBY DABBA DOO
Environmentally & Ecologically Sustainable Farming

CATCH & RELEASE OR BUY WHAT YOU CATCH!

BIRTHDAY PARTIES, SCHOOL GROUPS & CORPORATE FUN DAYS WELCOMED.

Clean old clothes, hat, water bottle & closed footwear essential. Don't forget the Aerogard!
Children must be accompanied by a responsible adult.

**WELCOME TO BRING A PICNIC LUNCH
STAY AS LONG AS YOU LIKE
BIOSECURITY CONDITIONS APPLY**

**123 SWAN BAY ROAD, KARUAH
NEW SOUTH WALES 2324**
PLEASE CHECK OUR WEBSITE FOR BIOSECURITY PROCEDURES

CRAY-Z COMPANIES

COME SEE WHAT WE YABBY DABBA DOO!

COME SEE WHAT IT'S ALL ABOUT WITH OUR FARM TOURS

If you are seriously considering Yabby Farming as a second income stream or stand alone business? This tour is for you!

YABBY FARM TOURS
60-90mins

TOPICS COVERED IN COMMERCIAL FARM TOURS INCLUDE:

Stocking Densities, Feed / Nutrition
Pond Size, Design & Pond Management
Production & Harvesting
Marketing & Shipping
Purging & Permits

BOOK A TOUR

Learn all about Yabby Farming in a 30+ Min guided tour of our Commercial Yabby Farm. Tours by appointment only.

LEARN ALL ABOUT YABBIES

Where they grow
What they eat
Identifying the sexes
Methods of catching

INCLUDES A TOUR OF OUR GROWING PONDS & PURGING FACILITY

(If you're game enough, you can even pick one up)

EFTPOS AVAILABLE - BOOKINGS ESSENTIAL

For more information including prices, check out our website:

YABBYDABBADOO.AU

PLEASE BE SURE TO READ OUR YABBY DOOS & DON'TS.
MENTION TTMARRON101 WHEN MAKING YOUR BOOKING.

PASES AQUA - W.A.

PASES AQUA

PASES AQUA IS A DIVERSE NATURE BASED SERVICE BUSINESS SPECIALISING IN A WIDE RANGE OF AQUATIC SERVICES;

NATURAL & ARTIFICIAL ECOSYSTEMS
- WETLANDS
- LAKES
- NATURAL POOLS
- PONDS
- AQUARIUMS
- AQUACULTURE
- AQUAPONICS

WE ALSO SUPPLY
- BLUE YABBIES
- BLUE MARRON
- POND PRODUCTS
- PUMPS, FILTERS & UV CLARIFIERS
- LAKE PRODUCTS
- AERATION SYSTEMS
- FOUNTAINS
- LAKE BED AERATORS
- SOLAR AERATORS

NO. 2/9 MERINO ENTRANCE
COCKBURN CENTRAL
WESTERN AUSTRALIA 6164
WWW.PASESAQUA.COM.AU

GOING THROUGH THE PASES

Our goal is to be the company that best understands and improves the quality of Aquatic systemsn whether it is a Wetland, Lake, Natural Pool, Pond, Aquaponics or Aquarium. We now have the largest aquatic based service team in W.A. with over 5 key staff and several sub-contractors.

Our business caters to a diverse range of clients from homeowners to commercial, industrial & government customers. **PASES Aqua** provides Aquaponics design consultations for residential & commercial clients, to ensure the design is viable, practical & enviromentally sustainable.

AQUAPONICS SERVICES

Aquaponics integrates the disciplines of both Aquaculture and Hydroponics to grow fish & plants symbiotically within an artifically built system. The advantage is you save water & reduce the need to add fertilizers or chemicals. The most common system uses a main tank to grow edible fish species. The water from this tank is pumped into a smaller tank (or grow bed) above, which contains vegetables overlaid by medium-sized clay media. An outlet on the bottom of the top tank allows percolation of the water through filter media (via gravity) to the bottom tank. In the process, waste excreted from fish provides nutrients for vegetables to grow. The fish benefit from filtered, nutrient-free clean water.

PASES Aqua can offer small-scale residential design services, commercial farm design service, pre-purchase inspections, evaluations & production forecasts.

To find out more: www.pasesaqua.com.au

MERV COOPERS CRAZY CRABS - W.A.

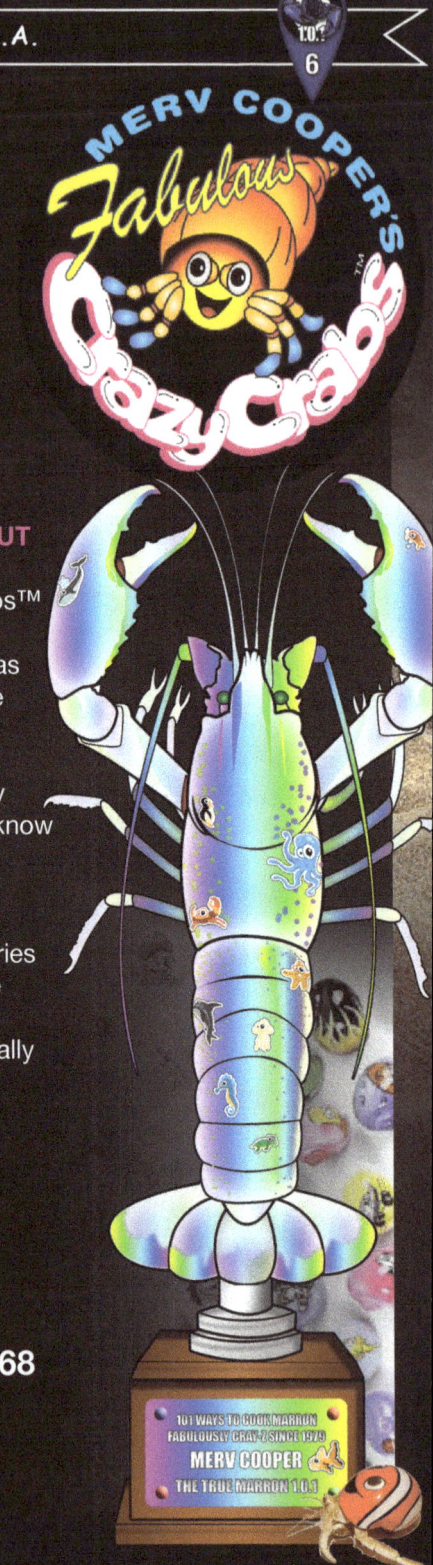

Does your child like crayfish but you don't want to risk the water in your home?
Get your young Astacologists started with our Mud-Bugs' Land-Cousin **THE HERMIT CRAB** *Paguroidea. (pag-ewe-ro-idea)*, Seems like a good idea to me too!

Friendly Reminder:
THEY CAN'T EAT THESE ONES!
Just ask Merv about Crazy Crabs™, he'll simply tell you!
"A HOME IS NOT A HOME WITHOUT A CRAZY CRAB"
The original and the best Crazy Crabs™ established in Perth W.A. in 1979. Crazy Crabs™ is a trademark and has become a household name for these lovable & adorable pets.
All our crabs are collected in North-Western Australia and over the many years we love our Crazy Crabs and know all about them.

Check out the funky range of hand painted shells, crabariums, accessories & food which we make on site at the **'CRAB SHACK'** in an assortment of designs, High gloss finish & individually hand painted.

COME TO THE
'CRAB SHACK'
**12 AMBROSE STREET,
ROCKINGHAM
WESTERN AUSTRALIA 6168
(+618) 9528 CRAB (2722)**

CRAY-Z COMPANIES

ATTENTION!
SCHOOL TEACHERS & FUND-RAISING COMMITTEES

WE OFFER CRAZY CRABS FOR SCHOOL FUNDRAISERS IN AND AROUND PERTH.
(Call to enquire if we can deliver to your location)

If your school is having a fête or fair to raise funds for school projects like library equipment, computers, school trips, etc, perhaps we can help!
Having Crazy Crabs at your fundraiser is a fun way to make some great money for your school.
We provide a Glass Aquarium for your Stall, Crazy Crabs, Carry Boxes, Crazy Crab Chow, Salt Bath Crystals, Spare Shells, Information Books & Plastic Tanks.

ALL AT WHOLESALE PRICES TO THE SCHOOL OR COMMITTEE!

CONTACT US TODAY
(08) 9528 CRAB (2722)
FOR MORE INFORMATION GO TO:
WWW.CRAZYCRABS.COM.AU

WHAT A GREAT WAY TO HAVE SOME FUN & MAKE MONEY FOR YOUR SCHOOL!

IT'S NOT THAT CRAY-Z MERV!

SEND US AN EMAIL FOR OUR PRICELIST
MERV@CRAZYCRABS.COM.AU

CRAY-Z COMPANIES

WOODVALE FISH & LILY FARM - W.A.

NOT ONLY DO WE HAVE THE FRIENDLIEST STAFF IN THE INDUSTRY! We **ALSO** stock a wide variety of traps & nets, perfect for harvesting Marron & Yabbies (For home & private use only)

Our pride on our range of fish nets, fish food and water control treatments is available online:
WOODVALEFISHLILYFARM.COM.AU

MARRON & YABBY HIDES - SAFETY IN LAYERS

Ideal for growing & harvesting Marron & Yabbies in backyard ponds. With a float at one end (included) & a weight at the other (not included), this allows the netting to sit diagonallyv or vertically in the water, therefore giving more places for the crustaceans to hide. They will not be confined to the base of the pond, with more space to move about there will be less fighting.
These hides will also make harvesting easier as all you have to do is pull it out & remove the crustaceans from the netting.
Stretches to 1m long x 60cm wide.

CRAY-Z COMPANIES

MARRON FOR SALE WITH HINTS & TIPS

- Water temp no higher than 22°C, provide shade on warm days
- Add plenty of hiding places (ie: PVC pipe, pots, mesh hides)
- Prefer a gravel base in pond/tank
- Protect pump cables from claws - Wrap with conduit / hose
- Feed with marron pellets - Approx. 1 pellet per animal per day
- Marron will climb out - You may need to cover top with netting
- Marron are omnivorous, they will eat fish if they can catch them
- Most vulnerable when shedding - Don't move or touch them
- Stocking rate 50-60 per 1000lt with good filtration & oxygen

YABBIES FOR SALE WITH HINTS & TIPS

- Water temp no higher than 22°C, provide shade on warm days
- Add plenty of hiding places (ie: PVC pipe, pots, mesh hides)
- Prefer a gravel base in pond/tank
- Protect pump cables from claws - Wrap with conduit / hose
- Feed with marron pellets - Approx. 1 pellet per animal per day
- Marron will climb out - You may need to cover top with netting
- Marron are omnivorous, they will eat fish if they can catch them
- Most vulnerable when shedding - Don't move or touch them
- Stocking rate 50-60 per 1000lt with good filtration & oxygen

THE MARRON GROWERS ASSOCIATION OF W.A.

The Association works to represent, inform, support and assist Marron growers and those looking to set up commercial marron growing on whatever scale. We workwith local, state and federal government departments to represent the views of our members and provide a forum for discussion that serves the best interests of the industry as a whole and the enviroments in which we operate.

Our website brings together a wealth of experience drawn from our members to provide a focal point for our educational efforts to assist new growers start up in the industry and existing growers to improve their production through research and shared experience.

**WHY NOT JOIN THE ASSOCIATION TODAY
AND HELP US SHAPE OUR INDUSTRY FOR THE FUTURE.**

OUR PRINCIPLES:
The principal objects of the Association are:
- To unite all persons in growing marron for their common benefit
- To collect and record information and facts relating to the breeding of marron
- To advertise & publicise such facts as it may from time to time in the opinion of the Committee be beneficial to the interests of the members to do so.

To fulfil these and other objects the Association has been instrumental in initiation various legislation changes which have allowed the number of aquaculture licences for marron farming to grow from 30 in 1994 to in excess of 250 today.
The Association holds Field Days for members and non-members (fee for non-members payable on the day to cover refreshments), along with workshops and seminars on various aspects of growing marron. We publish a Marron Growers Bulletin as well as e-newsletters for members.

A MANUAL FOR GROWERS

Marron Aquaculture in Western Australia - A Manual for Growers is an extensive practical guide for anyone who is starting up or investing in marron farming in Western Australia, and for existing marron growers who wish to expand their productivity. Whether you are a hobby farmer, large Marron producer, government department or just have an interest in Marron you will find this Marron manual essential reading.

ORDER YOUR COPY TODAY

PO Box 964 Manjimup, Western Australia 6258
E: secretary@marrongrowers.org   W: www.marrongrowers.org

MARRON GROWERS ASSOCIATION
OF WESTERN AUSTRALIA

CRAY-Z COMPANIES

```
A C E C M S V W T F G O X D W R U A W R N I
R H R I U P I P T I D O X O R O A R E A S W
E E C A S D R F L E F M Z A R N L T A G B C
H R P V S S E G E M N S M O R M Y T G R O R
C A O P Q S I R Q Q F U B Q E E E N N A R E
X X A K E E I I O J A S I Y V N H B E M O B
A W E A G N E M J D N E K M A N G C R V U A
E L O P L A W C A U U L R O A B D A O L G L
R X A R E H C Y D N E E I O O N B E E O H G
I Z U Y N A H W U Y U K S D O N U Y R W E W
Y I V I I I E Z R C Z S X P X M A S Y I A A
Q P N K R R R M I G E O Y K D I L C G I M L
F A U I E Y A C H E R A X V Y A H L P R O P
J S V V A R X R E D U C T A N T I L F X O O
C E I K R C H E R A X L D W E G L O I D R L
R R Y O S U T A N I R A C E U Q N I U Q E E
G C N H G U O R O B S N U D L E W P D D D A
D E S T R U C T O R V A E E C R A Y F I S H
C A N O O K S T Y C H E R A X H L B K V R D
D S U T A N I R A C I R D A U Q C I J L K K
```

CRAY-Z FIND A WORD – OVER AND OVER AGAIN!

CAINII	AREA	CRASSIMANUS
CHERAX	CHERAX	DIL
CLAW	CRAYFISH	CHERAX
DESTRUCTOR	DIL	DUNSBOROUGH
DIL	DUNSBOROUGH	ENGAEWA
DUNSBOROUGH	ENGAEWA	GILGIE
ENQAEWA	GILGIE	HAIRY
GLABER	KOONAC	CHERAX
CHERAX	CHERAX	MARGARET
KOONAC	MARRON	MOORE
MARRON	QUADRICARINATUS	PSEUDOREDUCTA
PREISSII	REDUCTA	RED
QUINQUECARINATUS	RIVER	RIVER
RIVER	WALPOLE	TENUIMANUS
SMOOTH	CHERAX	CHERAX
WALPOLEA		YABBY

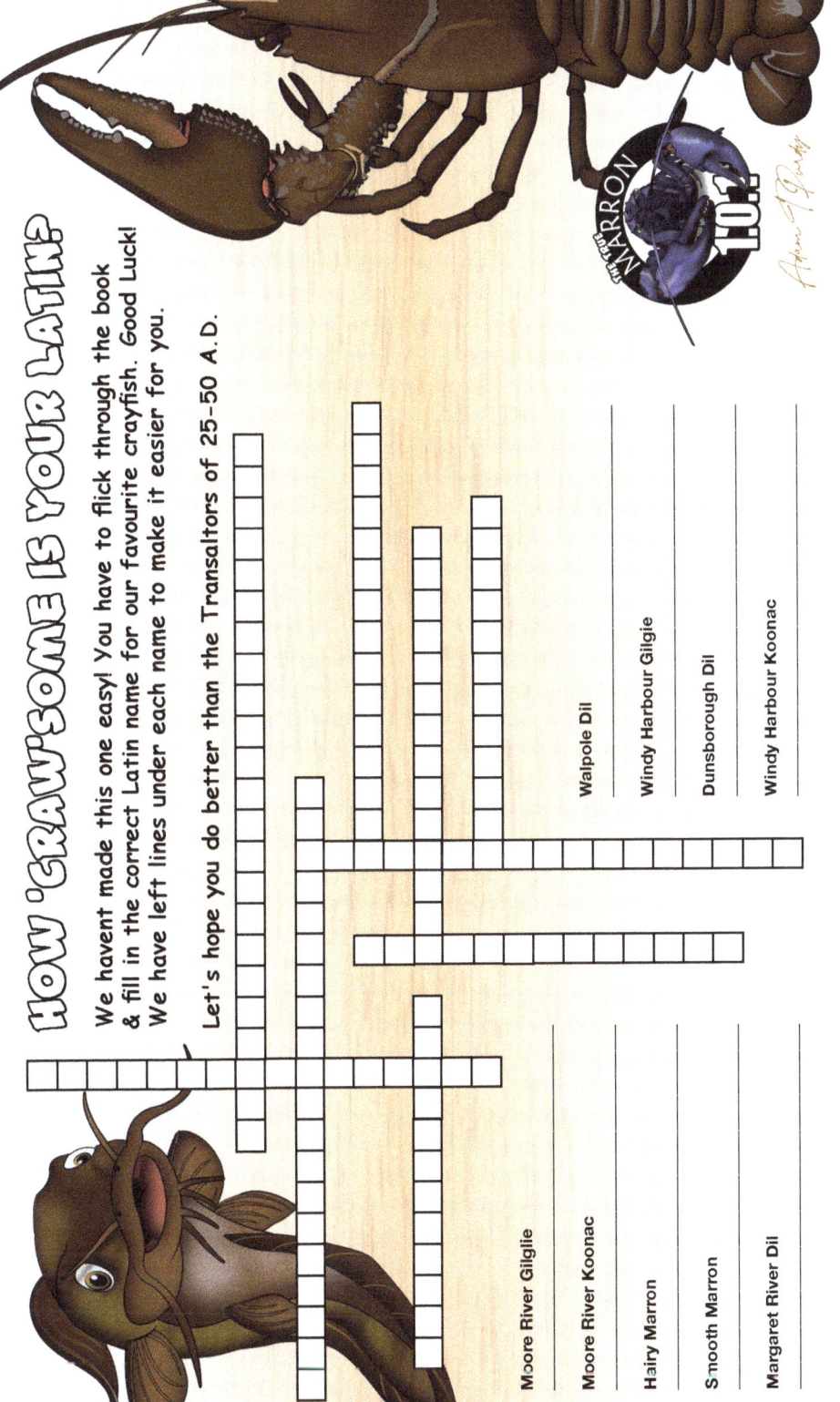

RESEARCH MEMBERS

**101 WAYS TO COOK MARRON
PARTICIPATION AWARD
ANTHONY EDWARDS
THE TRUE MARRON 1.0.1**

RESEARCH MEMBERS

'CRABBI' THE AQUA'COP'TER

Jump on our website thetruemarron101.au to keep up-to-date with our **'OFF'** the road research. The crew will be exploring Western Australia's Aquifers in search of Hairy Marron and burrowing Dil habitat.

The Yarragadee Formation is a **MAJOR REGIONAL AQUIFER** that extends for roughly 150km North from the south-coast of Western Australia and spans 40km wide!

Fresh oxegenated water is confined within the aquitard & aquiclude layers with a neutral PH level at the natural springs around the Manjimup Region and down towards **SHANNON NATIONAL RESERVE**. This will be updated as we travel the lower South-West studying the large quantity of natural springs we have and match that with underground aquifer systems that lay between Margaret River and the Bremer Basin.

The goal is to find underground pockets that could still be home to our local species of Cherax and Engaewa.

By using a dropline camera we can explore the surface entrance of the natural springs for signs of deeper caverns underneath of permeable rocks, sandstone and other porous materials. Water is easily able to move around in this drenched storage area and so are the crayfish.

If an entrance of a water cavern is found through the Aquitard layer with the dropline camera, we can explore deeper while staying safe on top of the surface.

'CRABBI' THE AQUA'COP'TER (Underwater Drone - Our **'ROBOT'** Friend) will record everything it sees, giving us clear footage of the crays beneath our feet.

Once a pocket of our **'ENDANGERED SPECIES'** have been found we can secure that area for future breeding plans.

As Hairy Marron require colder climates and are known for their large sizes. The Aquifers would make perfect breeding deposits as they get little sunlight and crayfish absorb their nutrients through the aerated water. Not to mention **'WELL'** out of human hands.

We have a way of over complicating things and 9 times out of 10, human interferrance does more damage than good!

Just look at the history of **EVERY** animal with medicinal purposes, including Rhino horn.

Seems science is only good as the pay cheque funding the research. The goal is to **LOCK DOWN** these locations to protect our waterways and aquifers, for our natural water cleaners and our future generations.

Let us all hope our combined efforts will protect our freshwater aquifers for the future generations to come!

> I 'HERD' IT THROUGH THE GRAPEVINE!

'JEEP' 'JEEP'

HOW CAN YOU HELP 'CRABBI' & ELI?

Nothing spreads faster than rumours and stories past down through our family and friend '**GRAPE-VINES**', not to mention the good ol' bar bench yarn you over'**HERD**' someone say! These unique information chains are not available for the University and Government funded programs.

No-one knows your backyard like you and we are asking for you to jump onto our website and send us a chat if you know of any wells (man-made natural spring entrances) locations and freshwater aquifers. Our crew would love to come out and meet you and have your information added to our research and the following book.

ON THE HUNT FOR THE TRUE MARRON

As this book has been a self-funded hobby since 2002, and from support from our **CRAY-Z COMPANIES** we are able to keep the research mobile and up-to-date and accessible by everybody. So we have created a merchandise range for our fans. Feels good to get something for your money whilst still donating to a good cause.

IT'S NOT THAT CRAY-Z!

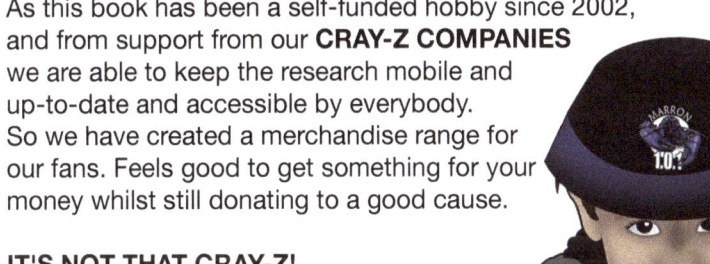

WELL, WELL, IT'S AN AQUIFER!

Ever since I was a child growing up in Manjimup, Western Australia. We were lucky enough to of lived a 'stones throw' from the local school & 'two stone throws' from our favourite Gilgie spot.

When playing with a friend one day we found a roundish shaped hole in the swampy marsh. Being a hot summer day in the lower South-West we decided we would jump in for a quick dip. It turned out to be deeper than we had thought. Upon this realisation, we got out, went home and came back with a rope. Grabbing a decent size flat rock we tied the double knot and lowered it down into the depths. After a few metres of rope had disappeared we had realised we had come across a well or something? We weren't too sure, all we knew was it became a race to get to the bottom.. After plunging into the dark water my friend & I '**DUCKDOVE**' and swam as hard as we could to the bottom. The water was dark, looking up made it look like we had swam forever. A few metres down we came to what we could guess to be the bottom. Both sitting in a cross-legged position and egg-beating the water with our hands we sat for as a long as our lungs would allow and kicked off to head back to surface. As our heads surfaced, my friend turned to me and said "Did you feel that?" We had both experienced a slight pull of the water as if it was a going down a slow blocked drain. So I quickly replied with an excited "Sure Did!"

After a bit of time at school I had quickly learnt of Aquifers and the Fresh-water Caverns of the South-West that lay under our feet.. Literally. Every winter, before school we would have to trudge through ankle deep sewerage water for the morning firewood. The Aquifers under our feet filled and over-flowed the septic tank giving our gum boots a nice coating of septic slime (Creating **STINKY KANKLES**).

Now, you may be sitting there saying? "Is this Guy saying we have football ovals full of water under our feet? What a tool!" Right? But Yes, after years of research and I came across the Yarragadee Formation Aquifer (More about that over the page).

Looking back and how it impacted my life as a career option, finding our local crayfish using the underground cavern systems to spread and as a discovered habitat option for our endangered crays, or perhaps adapted underground versions of their above ground cousins? Yabbies have been found 80km away from where they where deposited and burrows over 5 metres deep... Either way, it makes these underground eco-systems ever-so more vital and needing protection from being used by large Corporations & Mines.

HOPEFULLY THIS TIME KARKINOS ISN'T FIGHTING ALONE?

ROOM FOR A 'HOLE' FAMILY

RESEARCH MEMBERS

ARE THERE CRAYFISH IN OUR DRINKING WATER?

YES! They are made as natural water prufiers. Surely you cannot believe Chlorine is the best thing to clean water? Aquifers and Underground water systems are more common than you may think. We've all heard the stories about our grand-parents getting water from the well. It seemed to be a never ending supply of water just a bucket and a ropes throw away. There are many different forms of Aquifer. The lower South-West has granite beds and large limestone deposits scattered all throughout the area. This can create cavernous areas large enough for pocket ecosystems to thrive in the ever moving sludge and aerated water. Some of these passage ways may need a little ground work to find and make room for an underwater drone to access and investigate the water pockets. The amount of water that is stored in an aquifer can vary over the seasons, aquifers can gain water at a rate as much as 50 feet per year to as low as 50 inches per century. As aquifers have both Entry and Exit points for water. An Entry (**RECHARGE ZONE**) usually occurs at a high topographic elevation where rain, lake or river water seeps into the ground to making its way into the aquifer. An Exit (**DISCHARGE ZONE**) can happen anywhere. Natural springs, wetlands and streams can all be areas where the aquifer is losing water. Based on the pull we felt at the bottom of the Well as kids, I now know it was an Entry point to the aquifer under the Eastern Hills of Manjimup. The local school has made advantage of the area and turned it into a **KIDS CREEK PLAY** Area, taking advantage of the natural spring arising from the previous hillside. Which I am sure you can imagine, after 40 years that natural spring still feeds the local kids their weekend adventures hunting gilgies with their friends.

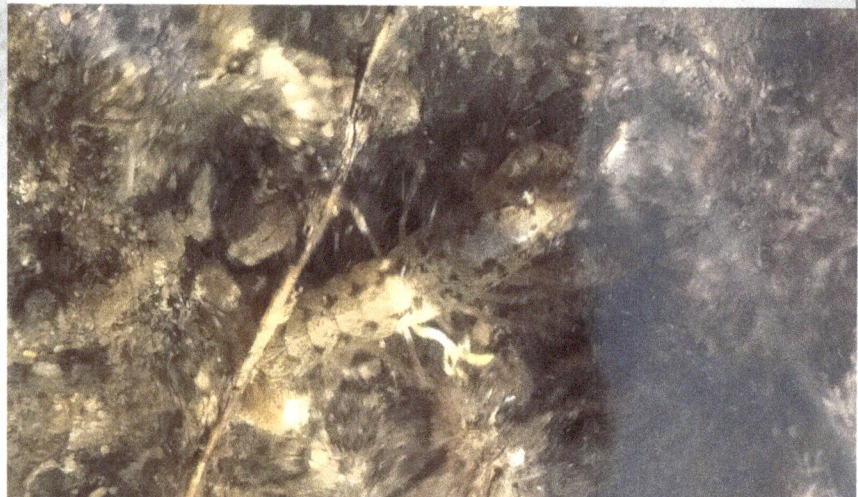

WATER TABLE

**UNCONFINED AQUIFER
SEDIMENTARY LAYER**

**AQUITARD
GRANITE & LIMESTONE**

**CONFINED AQUIFER
BETWEEN LAYERS**

**AQUICLUDE
BEDDED CHURT & SALT STONE**

THE TWO TYPES OF AQUIFER

There are two types of aquifer by standard definition; confined and unconfined: A confined aquifer happens when water in porous layers is trapped by layers that are reasonably solid, like granite or dense clay deposits. Confined layers tend to be under pressure and typically are underground watercavern systems. (**IMAGINE GIANT WORM HOLES, IT HELPS**.) Unconfined layers are where ground water islocated. This is water right under the soil, the top of this is considered the water table. Most people with wells on their properties are tapping into an unconfined aquifer.

With the industrial age bringing in fertilisers and chemicals, this could lead to the well being contaminated and **NEAR ON IMPOSSIBLE TO REVIVE THE DRINKING WATER** on the farm, obviously killing any crustacean and other life along with it.

Do you have a Well or Natural Spring close to where you live? You will always find them teaming with life and micro-organisims. See them as the **ENTRY** and **EXIT** ramps to an underground world teaming with crustaceans all trying to keep your water clean for you.

The more we do to help to remove chemicals out of our lives, the more chance natures forbidden scavengers have of regenerating their numbers in the future.

WHAT HAPPENS WHEN THEY STOP 'CRAW'LING?

Australia's Mud-Bugs have had the eye of the world on them for decades as we have some of the worlds fastest growing freshwater crayfish in the world. Saying that! We also have some of the slowest growing too!

As Australia is a country of vast climatic differences not just between states, but in the unique hydrozones that each individual species of cray have adapted to and can thrive in without the threat of invading species.

The role the freshwater cray plays in each ecosystem as detritivores can easy go unrecognised by the average 'Joe Blowfish'. Where in fact crayfish they are quite the underwater farmers. They plow and regenerate the soils extracting all the impurities leaving us with clean spring water. The people of the land always said **"IF THERE ARE CRAY IN THERE!, YOU CAN DRINK IT!"**.

But what happens when crays are removed from an enviroment? Karkinos Astactus II explained what happened to his family in Sweden after the plague in '64. "Plant growth took over the pond and the water became riddled with leeches, molluscs and frogs. It was terrible" he explained."Tadpoles ate the fish eggs, The Leech Squad attacked all our friends, either driving them out of the pond or draining their body of all its blood while they slept.. No mask was going to save us from this disease. The town folk soon came to understand our benefits for not just our incredible farming skills in the waterways, but our ability of ridding the ponds of **ACTUAL PESTS!** The ones that want your water to be contaminated, undrinkable, dirty, full of carcass decay and generally unusable." Sounds like he's talking about a corporation not a leech.. personally!

SO? WHO'S LOOKING AFTER WHO?

"Karkinos Astacus Astacus the First. (My Father) told me about the day he nipped Hercules on his **KANKLE.**" he continued "What the Westerners don't tell you is that '**MR DEVINE BEING**' himself was littering and searching for new locations to syphon water for his palace, he deserved to be put in his place!
I don't go to his home and drop my 'Snigger Bar' wrappers everywhere! He wanted to drill holes to extract water for Zues's water features and marble carvings.
Dad wouldn't of minded if he didn't come in stomping his '**HERO**' feet all over the banks destroying homes. Zues's Palace would of drained **950,000 TONNES** per year to run just one of his fountains and he wanted to rig it to run 12! That would be catastrophic above and below the surface. If levels in aquifers are affected dramatically it can create sink holes and cause underground quakes as levels rise and fall. Not to mention the endangered cray species that may be finding home not just in the seimentary layer but also deeper in the depths of the aquifer itself.

**THE BIGGEST MUST LOOK AFTER THE SMALLEST..
BUT SEEMS THIS TIME IT'S THE OTHER WAY AROUND!**

WHAT HAPPENS IF HERCULES WINS AGAIN?

A large portion of the world's fresh water resides underground, stored within cracks and pores in the rock that make up the Earth's crust. Majority of the population rely on ground water for domestic ie; drinking, irrigation, industry, and livestock. This is particularly true in areas with limited rainfall, surface water resources, or high demand from agriculture and growing populations. Some eco-systems such as wetlands or surface waters fed by springs, also rely on ground water.

IF HE TAKES WHAT HE WANTS? TO WHAT EXTENT?

The extent of ground water refers to the amount available? typically it is measured in terms of volume, or saturated thickness of an aquifer (body of ground water). Concerns related to extent include aquifer depletion and excessive ground water in aquifers.

AQUIFER DEPLETION.
Factors that can deplete aquifers include changes in rain & snow fall patterns; withdrawal of ground water for drinking, irrigation, and other human uses; and impervious paved surfaces that prevent precipitation (rain & snowfall) from recharging ground water. Some of the deep aquifers may take thousands of years to replenish.

SOME CONSEQUENCES OF AQUIFER DEPLETION INCLUDE:
LOWER LAKE LEVELS are a major result, in extreme cases intermittent or totally dry perennial streams. These effects can harm aquatic and river plants and animals that depend on regular surface flows.

LAND SUBSIDENCE & SINKHOLE FORMATION in areas of heavy withdrawal. (these effects are already quite noticeable around the lower South-West). These changes can damage buildings, roads, and other structures and can permanently reduce aquifer recharge capacity by compacting the aquifer medium (soil or rock).

SALT WATER INTRUSION can cause changes in ground water flow and lead to saline ground water migrating into aquifers previously occupied by fresh ground water.

TOO MUCH GROUND WATER. Some human activities, such as pumping water into the ground for oil and gas extraction, can cause an aquifer to hold too much ground water. Too much ground water discharge to streams can lead to erosion and alter the balance of aquatic plant and animal species.

THE CHANGING OF GROUND WATER CONDITIONS

Stressors that affect ground water condition include application of pesticides and fertilizers to the land, waste from livestock and other animals, landfills, mining operations, and unintentional releases such as chemical spills or leaks from storage tanks. Some ground water has high levels of naturally occurring dissolved solids (salinity), or metals such as arsenic found in natural rock formations.

THESE STRESSORS CAN ULTIMATELY AFFECT:
The quality of water available for drinking, irrigation, or other human needs. Treatment may be needed to ensure that finished drinking water does not pose risks to human OR other species of animals' health. Many fish species depend on spring-fed waters for habitat or spawning grounds. Aquifers themselves can constitute an ecosystem, such as caves and sinkholes that support invertebrates and fish adapted to life underground. These are what we need to put our focus into protecting, not **'POND'**sy Schemes.
The extent and condition of ground water are often intertwined. Stressors that affect the extent of ground water—such as withdrawal or injection of the water out of the aquifer—can change ground water velocity and flow. These physical changes can affect patterns of discharge to surface waters and the movement of water and contaminants within the ground.

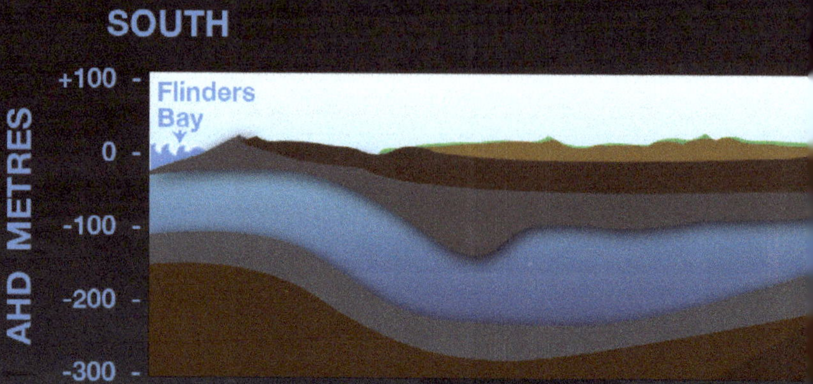

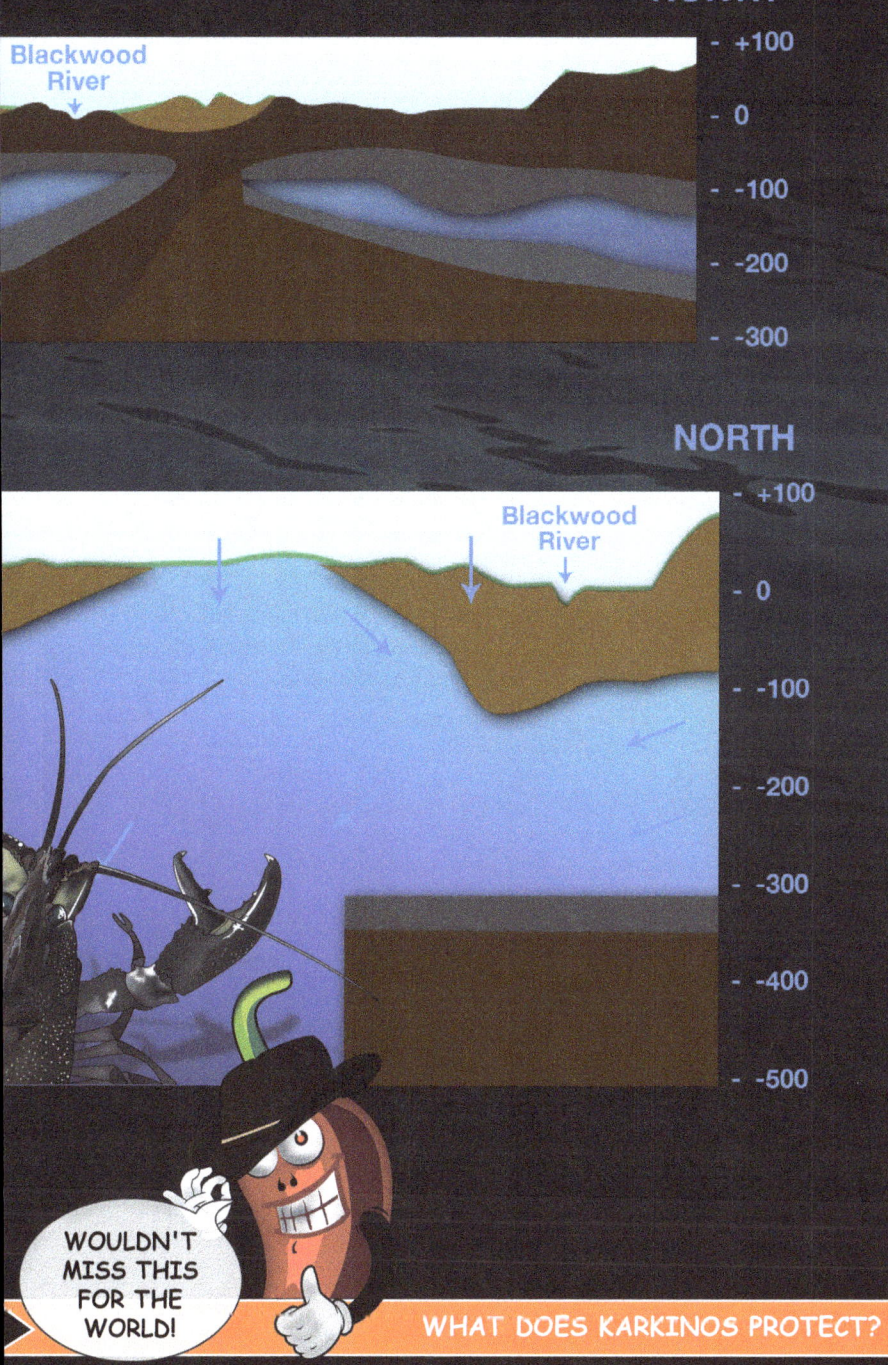

NATURE CONSERVATION PARTNERS & SUPPORTERS

Nature Conservation seeks to leverage the strength of the regional community by raising awareness, inspiring commitment and empowering action on behalf of the environment.
To this end it develops and nurtures a diverse network of supporters within the Margaret River region. This includes strong grassroots support from individuals and local businesses, teams of dedicated volunteers and citizen scientists, a network of strategic partnerships as well as collaborative working relationships with Federal, State, and local government agencies.

THREATENED SPECIES PROTECTION

Nature Conservation is working to protect many unique species currently at risk in the Margaret River region include the critically endangered Western Ringtail Possum, Margaret River Hairy Marron & three species of black cockatoos, the Carnaby, Baudins and Red Tailed Black Cockatoos. Threatened native fish species are also a focus as an indicator of the ecological health of our waterways. Through partnerships with State government agencies, local government and organisations such as Birdlife WA and in accordance with recovery plans for these species Nature Conservation focuses on raising public awareness of conservation status, increasing understanding of species distribution through citizen science surveying & assisting with onground conservation action where necessary.

ENVIRONMENTAL EDUCATION

The '**OUR PATCH**' Environmental Education Program delivered by Nature Conservation increases ecological awareness through engagement with nature and involvement in local conservation issues and programs. The program fosters our future environmental stewards inspiring children to value, respect and care for nature. '**OUR PATCH**' currently works with over 500 Year 3 & Year 6 students from 8 local primary schools in the region. Another Nature Conservation program, '**ADOPT A SPOT**', connects local schools to an area of bushland, river foreshore or coastline in the region. This further connects young people with nature and engages school communities in long term environmental restoration projects and forms long term partnerships with local 'Friends of Reserve' volunteer groups.

WWW.NATURECONSERVATION.ORG.AU

CALLING ALL CITIZEN SCIENTISTS & NATURE GURUS

Any one can join a citizen science project and be a citizen scientist! Citizen science projects in the Margaret River region are designed to find out more about our threatened fauna. Where do they occur? How many individuals are there? Are populations increasing, decreasing or stable? Are they disappearing from some areas? Data collected through these projects are used to answer specific research questions and can assist in policy and management decisions for the Margaret River region. It is invaluable to know the status of our threatened fauna in the region and to be able to take positive actions to protect them.

When you join a citizen science project you will be able to share your skills, learn new skills and have the opportunity to enjoy positive encounters with our local fauna. Check out our website to see our current research projects and how you can help;
WWW.MARGARETRIVERCONSERVATIONCENTRE.COM.AU

One part of our research we would **LOVE TO RE-OPEN** is our **MARGARET RIVER HAIRY MARRON RESEARCH** and/or find any subspecies in different hydrozones.

The Margaret River Hairy Marron (Cherax tenuimanus) is a critically endangered aquatic species found only in the Margaret River. The Margaret River Hairy Marron differs from introduced smooth marron because of the presence of small hairs (setae) on its hard upper shell. Wild populations of the Margaret River Hairy Marron are now restricted to a few river pools in the upper reaches of the Margaret River and total numbers in the wild are thought to be as low as 1000 individuals. Threats to this species include competition and interbreeding with the smooth marron, habitat disturbance and poaching.

WE NEED YOUR HELP! WE CANNOT BE IN EVERY CORNER TO FIND ANY REMAINING POCKETS OF DIL OR HAIRY MARRON.

TITLES: The-Scary-Hairy-decline-CS.pdf & Hairy-marron-community-update-Final-1.pdf

EAST MANJIMUP PRIMARY SCHOOL - W.A.

East Manjimup Primary School is a public school located in the town of Manjimup in the beautiful jarrah and karri forests of the South-West region of WA. The school site is 17.5 acres, surrounded on two sides by a farm and one side with remnant native jarrah forest. On the other side of the main road that passes the school is another stand of remnant native forest. The school caters for students in Kindergarten through to Year 6.

The school has a great focus on outdoor experiences and learning, including Natureplay playground, mountain biking, hiking, Bush Kindy and skateboarding.

A creek runs through the school property and this flows for the majority of months each year. Many years ago the parcel of land the creek runs through was cleared of trees and used as a horse paddock. The school, in partnership with some community organisations, continues to develop the creek site, removing weeds (especially blackberry), planting a range of native plants and doing earthworks where needed. Students and staff are involved in this work. In Term 3 of each year classes spend time in the creek area. We call this Creek Play and it is a very special and important annual experience for our school community. Students attend in class groups and have the opportunity to wade, swim, explore and play.

The children have plenty of opportunity to find and investigate various small creatures, including native crustaceans, frogs, fish and worms. All animals are returned to the locations they were found. In the course of playing in the creek area students have seen kangaroos, eagles, Carnaby's Black Cockatoos and a quenda (southern brown bandicoot) has also been spotted in the area.

WE CATCH KOONACS & GILGIES. WHAT'S IN YOUR CREEKS?

Students also make small dams; 'race' sticks and leaves in the flowing water; cover themselves with mud, and use fallen trees as bridges to cross the water. Creek Play is wonderfully supported by our parent body, with all students given permission to participate; a number of parents volunteering to assist, and much positive feedback given to the school from families.

The quality of the creek water is tested by the W.A Water Corporation. A staff member with appropriate swimming supervision qualifications is always in attendance.

Another highlight of Creek Play is the 'hosing' of the children. Students who return to the main school buildings in a muddy state (which means they haven't washed themselves off in the creek) have the pleasure of being hosed off under a garden hose. Considering it is July/August/September when Creek Play is held, the water is very cold yet there are plenty of students quite willing to undergo this experience.

The staff at East Manjimup Primary School believe outdoor play and learning, such as Creek Play, is beneficial and vital for children's wellbeing. In a world full of electronic screens we believe providing such opportunities is needed, and to see students enjoy and participate in Creek Play is so pleasing.

MICHAEL SMITH
E.M.P.S Principal 2022.

IT'S NOT JUST PLANTS YOU HELP GROW!
Thank You Mr Kelly!
FROM EVERY TEACHER, STUDENT & PARENT

CRAY-Z IS AS CRAY-Z DOES
THE TRUE MARRON 1.0.?

STUDYING THE NATURAL SPRINGS ON RAINBOW BEACH Q.L.D

MERCHANDISE PACKS FOR SALE*

ALL FUNDS RAISED WILL GO TO HELP WITH:
THE 1.0.1 'OFF' THE ROAD RESEARCH
(page 212)

PURCHASE FROM OUR EVER GROWING COLLECTION
OR HAVE YOUR OWN CUSTOMISED SHIRT DONE.

LET'S KEEP THE MEMORIES ALIVE!

USE THIS UNIVERSAL PROMO CODE:

IMCRAY-Z
AT THE CHECKOUT TO GET
20% OFF ALL PRODUCTS

THETRUEMARRON101.AU

REGISTER AS A RESEARCH MEMBER

Eli is trying to help Mazz find his friends around Australia & the World. Nearly every country have their own unique varieties. Australia alone has over 157 individual species of freshwater crayfish. Eli wants to meet them all!

Regardless of where we are from, I am sure most of us can remember going down to our local stream, creek, brook or esturary and moving a few rocks and watching little crayfish shoot out from under with one or two quick flicks of their tail. Those moments should not just be memories, but something we pass down to the future generations. No matter where we are from, everyone (besides the allergic and 'some' religious groups of course) come together around and a campfire sharing a feed of freshwater crayfish or have it included in their history and stories. We here in the lower South-West of Australia have two of our 11 species on the Critically Endangered list and it is obviously happening all over Australia and other countries as well. With regions being substantially altered by clearing of native vegetation to make way for an ever growing population. Not to mention the introductions of foreign cray species. All over the world are teams of university students and unpaid volunteer groups who need our information to help them track the growth and decrease in individual crayfish species habitats, they struggle with getting time to be out in the field and that's where you and your family can help.

The last few pages of the book are set up as a table as a generic data collection. We want to know what is happening in your region! so now's the time to put on your **BIG BLACK BOOTS** and take the family on an adventure exploring your local waterways.

As members grow we are looking at having a clear understanding on how quickly species can take over regions and what can be done to prevent these measures.

REGISTER YOUR FAMILY AS A RESEARCH GROUP

Fill out the registration form on the back page.
Providing your local research group you would like your collected data to go to. Provide registration fee receipt and address for member pack delivery. Cut it out and post to: P.O. Box 1045 Manjimup. Western Australia 6258 or email: adam@thetruemarron101.au. As numbers increase on data collected, http://thetruemarron101.au/ will provide awards reguarly to active participants. including merchandise, Amazon vouchers and custom designs of your chosen photo or competitor/s largest catches.

LET'S KEEP OUR MUD-BUGS GOING.

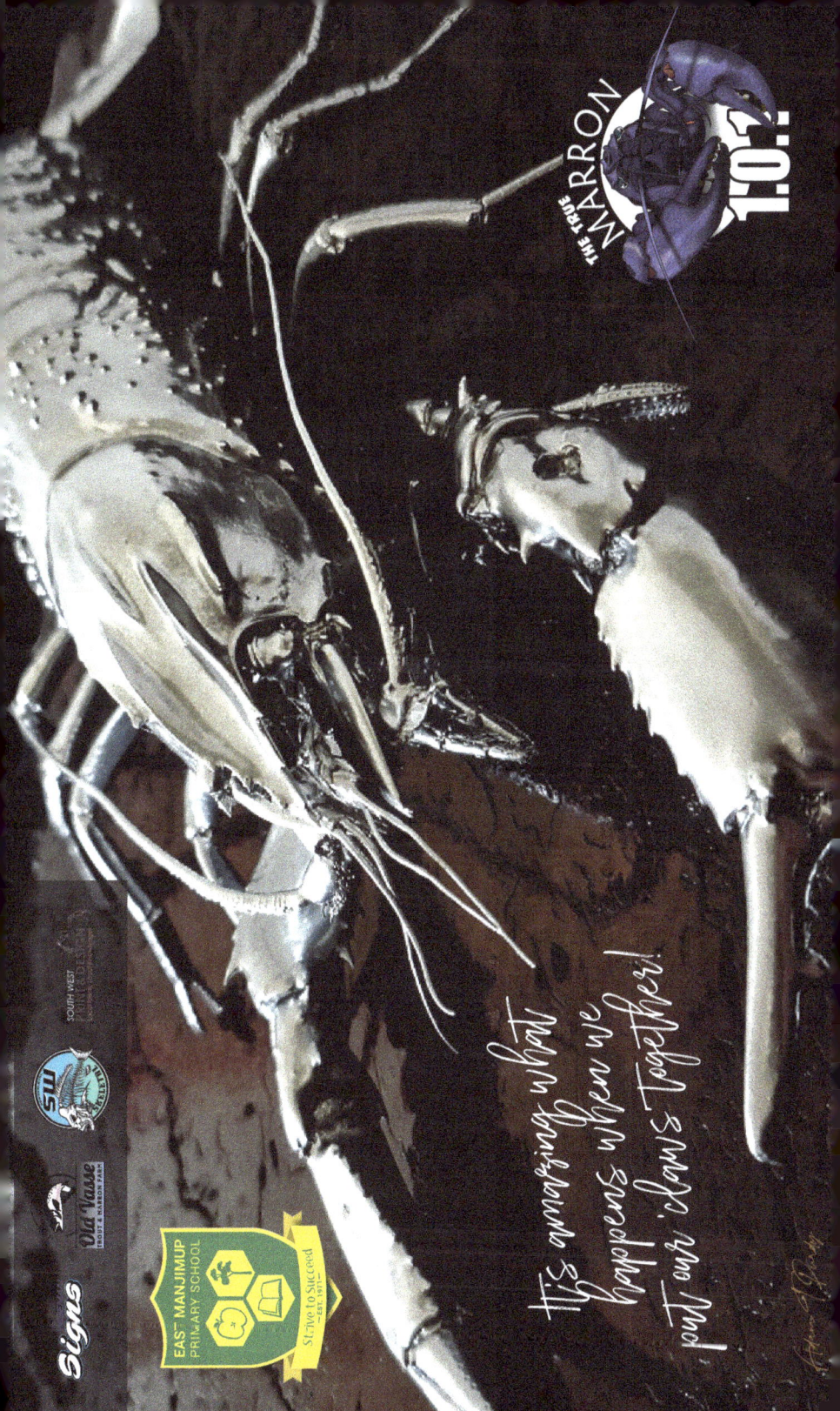

Let the Real Notes Begin!

Let the Real Notes Begin!

NAME OF STREAM, RIVER OR DAM (GPS Location if possible)	METHOD ie: Scoop Net, Drop nets, Snare, Lure.	What did you catch?				LENGTH OF BEST 2	COMMENTS OR SPECIES NAME eg: Type of bait, Weather conditions, Any in Berry, Disease affected.
		NATIVE SPECIES		PEST SPECIES			
		M	F	M	F		

Member ID No.: _____

Once you have filled out the sheets, please take a clear photograph of your completed sampling sheet and email to: adam@thetruemarron101.au

NAME OF STREAM, RIVER OR DAM (GPS Location if possible)	METHOD ie: Scoop Net, Drop nets, Snare, Lure.	What did you catch?		LENGTH OF BEST 2		COMMENTS OR SPECIES NAME eg: Type of bait, Weather conditions, Any in Berry, Disease affected.
		NATIVE SPECIES M / F	PEST SPECIES M / F			

Member ID No.: _____

Once you have filled out the sheets, please take a clear photograph of your completed sampling sheet and email to: adam@**thetruemarron101.au**

NAME OF STREAM, RIVER OR DAM (GPS Location if possible)	METHOD ie: Scoop Net, Drop nets, Snare, Lure.	What did you catch?		LENGTH OF BEST 2	COMMENTS OR SPECIES NAME eg: Type of bait, Weather conditions, Any in Berry, Disease affected.
		NATIVE SPECIES M / F	PEST SPECIES M / F		

Member ID No.:_____

Once you have filled out the sheets, please take a clear photograph of your completed sampling sheet and email to: adam@**thetruemarron101.au**

Page:____ of ____.

NAME OF STREAM, RIVER OR DAM (GPS Location if possible)	METHOD ie: Scoop Net, Drop nets, Snare, Lure.	What did you catch?		LENGTH OF BEST 2	COMMENTS OR SPECIES NAME eg: Type of bait, Weather conditions, Any in Berry, Disease affected.
		NATIVE SPECIES M / F	PEST SPECIES M / F		

Member ID No.: _____

Once you have filled out the sheets, please take a clear photograph of your completed sampling sheet and email to: adam@thetruemarron101.au

Page: ____ of ____ .

RESEARCH MEMBERSHIP APPLICATION

Let the Adventures Begin!

SOUTH WEST PRINT & DESIGN
Local Ideas, Local Knowledge!

LEAD RESEARCH MEMBER TO FILL

First Name: _____ Last Name: _____
Address: _____
Suburb: _____ State: _____ PC: _____
Contact number: _____ Email: _____

OTHER FAMILY TEAM MEMBERS: (Family MEMBERS ONLY)

First Name: _____ Last Name: _____
First Name: _____ Last Name: _____
First Name: _____ Last Name: _____
First Name: _____ Last Name: _____

CHOOSE YOUR PARTICIPATION LEVEL: (please tick to agree)

☐ I have found my local University or Research Organisation I would like my research to be available for. (details provided below)

_____ State: _____

☐ I am not aware of any local University doing any research but would like to assist in my region.

☐ I have attached a copy of my drivers licence for identification purposes only. (witnessed by a J.P. for legal purposes)

☐ I understand that if I or any of my Registered Team Members are caught doing the wrong thing, my membership ID Number will be withdrawn.

☐ I will share photos of crayfish species recorded for reference purposes to identify species if required to. Photos will be emailed with my **ID. REF. NO.** & Data Sheet to: **thetruemarron101@gmail.com**.

☐ I will keep my Research **ID. BADGE** on my person while assisting in our local freshwater crayfish research; either located inside the cover of the book or on the back window of my vehicle.

A FEE OF $30 IS REQUIRED TO BE PAID. THIS COST COVERS YOUR MERCHANDISE PACK AS STANDARD.

To submit your written application either: Photograph and email with a copy of your drivers licence (signed by J.P) to: thetruemarron101.au or post to: PO Box 1045 Manjimup WA 6258. Please include Money Order or Cheque for Registration Fee.

For the Tech Savvy! Jump Online, thetruemarron101.au and **REGISTER ONLINE!**

RESEARCH MEMBERSHIP APPLICATION

LEAD RESEARCH MEMBER TO FILL

SOUTH WEST
PRINT & DESIGN
Local Ideas, Local Knowledge!

First Name: _____ Last Name: _____
Address: _____
Suburb: _____ State: _____ PC: _____
Contact number: _____ Email: _____

OTHER FAMILY TEAM MEMBERS: (Family MEMBERS ONLY)

First Name: _____ Last Name: _____
First Name: _____ Last Name: _____
First Name: _____ Last Name: _____
First Name: _____ Last Name: _____

CHOOSE YOUR PARTICIPATION LEVEL: (please tick to agree)

☐ I have found my local University or Research Organisation I would like my research to be available for. (details provided below)

_____ State: _____

☐ I am not aware of any local University doing any research but would like to assist in my region.

☐ I have attached a copy of my drivers licence for identification purposes only. (witnessed by a J.P. for legal purposes)

☐ I understand that if I or any of my Registered Team Members are caught doing the wrong thing, my membership ID Number will be withdrawn.

☐ I will share photos of crayfish species recorded for reference purposes to identify species if required to. Photos will be emailed with my **ID. REF. NO.** & Data Sheet to: **thetruemarron101@gmail.com**.

☐ I will keep my Research **ID. BADGE** on my person while assisting in our local freshwater crayfish research; either located inside the cover of the book or on the back window of my vehicle.

A FEE OF $30 IS REQUIRED TO BE PAID. THIS COST COVERS YOUR MERCHANDISE PACK AS STANDARD.

To submit your written application either: Photograph and email with a copy of your drivers licence (signed by J.P) to: thetruemarron101.au or post to: PO Box 1045 Manjimup WA 6258. Please include Money Order or Cheque for Registration Fee.

For the Tech Savvy! Jump Online, thetruemarron101.au and **REGISTER ONLINE!**

CRIME INVESTIGATION SLEUTH THEORY - C.I.S.T FORM

CRIME COMMITTED:
Kidnap / Murder / Missing Persons
VICTIM NAME: Mazz Carcinos Cainii   **D.O.B** 03/02/1984
OCCUPATION: 'Craw'fessional chef
DESCRIPTION:
SPECIES: Red Marron   **SEX:** M / F / U
HEIGHT: 600mm   **WEIGHT:** 2kg

SPECIAL IDENTIFICATION MARKS:
Large Claws, 6 Legs (lost four in a net), Yellow-brown belly, Clean shaved (smooth). Always smiles.

Is there anything you can tell us to help us solve the case?
The accurate details will save a '**CRAB**'load of time for the office clergy.
PLEASE NOTE: Uncompleted forms will not be accepted).

LAST SEEN: (please fill in your selected recipe or title details)
_____ Page:_____

LAST SEEN WEARING:

_____ Page:_____

EXPLAIN YOUR THEORY: (accuracy counts with solving the case).
_____ Page:_____
_____ Page:_____
_____ Page:_____
_____ Page:_____
_____ Page:_____
_____ Page:_____
_____ Page:_____
_____ Page:_____
_____ Page:_____

IS THERE A SUSPECT?: (Please fill in details if required)
SUSPECTS FULL NAME: _____
ACCOMPLICE NAME1: _____
ACCOMPLICE NAME2: _____

YOUR NAME: _____   **SUBMITTED:** ___/___/_____

'SHELL'OCK IS ON THE CASE

SOUTH WEST MARRON

CRIME INVESTIGATION SLEUTH THEORY - C.I.S.T FORM

CRIME COMMITTED:
Kidnap / Murder / Missing Persons
VICTIM NAME: Mazz Carcinos Cainii   **D.O.B** 03/02/1984
OCCUPATION: 'Craw'fessional chef
DESCRIPTION:
SPECIES: Red Marron   **SEX:** M / F / U
HEIGHT: 600mm   **WEIGHT:** 2kg

SPECIAL IDENTIFICATION MARKS:
Large Claws, 6 Legs (lost four in a net), Yellow-brown belly, Clean shaved (smooth). Always smiles.

Is there anything you can tell us to help us solve the case?
The accurate details will save a '**CRAB**'load of time for the office clergy.
PLEASE NOTE: Uncompleted forms will not be accepted).

LAST SEEN: (please fill in your selected recipe or title details)
_____ Page:_____

LAST SEEN WEARING:
_____ Page:_____

EXPLAIN YOUR THEORY: (accuracy counts with solving the case).
_____ Page:_____
_____ Page:_____
_____ Page:_____
_____ Page:_____
_____ Page:_____
_____ Page:_____
_____ Page:_____
_____ Page:_____
_____ Page:_____

IS THERE A SUSPECT?: (Please fill in details if required)
SUSPECTS FULL NAME: _____
ACCOMPLICE NAME1: _____
ACCOMPLICE NAME2: _____

YOUR NAME: _____   **SUBMITTED:** ___/___/_____

'SHELL'OCK IS ON THE CASE

CRIME INVESTIGATION SLEUTH THEORY - C.I.S.T FORM

CRIME COMMITTED:
Kidnap / Murder / Missing Persons
VICTIM NAME: Mazz Carcinos Cainii   **D.O.B** 03/02/1984
OCCUPATION: 'Craw'fessional chef
DESCRIPTION:
SPECIES: Red Marron   **SEX: M / F / U**
HEIGHT: 600mm   **WEIGHT:** 2kg

SPECIAL IDENTIFICATION MARKS:
Large Claws, 6 Legs (lost four in a net), Yellow-brown belly, Clean shaved (smooth). Always smiles.

Is there anything you can tell us to help us solve the case?
The accurate details will save a '**CRAB**'load of time for the office clergy.
PLEASE NOTE: Uncompleted forms will not be accepted).

LAST SEEN: (please fill in your selected recipe or title details)
_____ Page:_____

LAST SEEN WEARING:

_____ Page:_____

EXPLAIN YOUR THEORY: (accuracy counts with solving the case).
_____ Page:_____
_____ Page:_____
_____ Page:_____
_____ Page:_____
_____ Page:_____
_____ Page:_____
_____ Page:_____
_____ Page:_____
_____ Page:_____

IS THERE A SUSPECT?: (Please fill in details if required)
SUSPECTS FULL NAME: _____
ACCOMPLICE NAME1: _____
ACCOMPLICE NAME2: _____

YOUR NAME: _____   **SUBMITTED:** ___/___/_____

'SHELL'OCK IS ON THE CASE

CRIME INVESTIGATION SLEUTH THEORY - C.I.S.T FORM

CRIME COMMITTED:
Kidnap / Murder / Missing Persons
VICTIM NAME: Mazz Carcinos Cainii **D.O.B** 03/02/1984
OCCUPATION: 'Craw'fessional chef
DESCRIPTION:
SPECIES: Red Marron **SEX: M / F / U**
HEIGHT: 600mm **WEIGHT:** 2kg

SPECIAL IDENTIFICATION MARKS:
Large Claws, 6 Legs (lost four in a net), Yellow-brown belly, Clean shaved (smooth). Always smiles.

Is there anything you can tell us to help us solve the case?
The accurate details will save a '**CRAB**'load of time for the office clergy.
PLEASE NOTE: Uncompleted forms will not be accepted).

LAST SEEN: (please fill in your selected recipe or title details)
_____ Page:_____

LAST SEEN WEARING:
_____ Page:_____

EXPLAIN YOUR THEORY: (accuracy counts with solving the case).
_____ Page:_____
_____ Page:_____
_____ Page:_____
_____ Page:_____
_____ Page:_____
_____ Page:_____
_____ Page:_____
_____ Page:_____
_____ Page:_____

IS THERE A SUSPECT?: (Please fill in details if required)
SUSPECTS FULL NAME: _____
ACCOMPLICE NAME1: _____
ACCOMPLICE NAME2: _____

YOUR NAME: _____ **SUBMITTED:** ___/___/_____

SHELLOCK IS ON THE CASE

FOLLOW US ON FACEBOOK
TO SECURE YOUR POSITION IN OUR NEXT PUBLICATION

We would love to have you on-board participating in this and helping us create this into something more!

101 ways to COOK MARRON & THE TRUE MARRON 1.0.1
ON THE HUNT FOR THE TRUE MARRON
SOUTH WEST PRINT & DESIGN

ABN: 39 493 180 942

www.ingramcontent.com/pod-product-compliance
Lightning Source LLC
Chambersburg PA
CBHW051535010526
44107CB00064B/2735